Total Clarity

Total Clarity

UNDERSTANDING THE FOUR KEYS
TO SUCCESSFUL INVESTING

By

Lucien A. Stephenson, CKA®

Printed in the United States of America

First Edition, Revised
ISBN-13: 9780692430118 (Custom Universal)
ISBN-10: 0692430113
Library of Congress Control Number: 2015906456
The Little Book on Giving, Dover, OH
BISAC: Business & Economics / Investments & Securities / Stocks
Author Contact:
Phone: 330-232-9199
Email: lucien@stephensoncompany.com

Table of Contents

The cover photo was taken from the bow of the Deep Blue II, a 46-foot catamaran operated by the Moorings Yacht Charter Company. The island in the background is Peter Island in the British Virgin Islands. Peter Island was the setting for Robert Louis Stevenson's book, "Treasure Island."

About the Author

LUCIEN A. STEPHENSON, CKA® IS President of *Stephenson & Company*, a Registered Investment Advisor (RIA), and an independent, fee-based wealth manager dedicated to exceeding the expectations of his clients.

He has the capability to deliver Socially Responsible Investing (SRI) as well as Biblically Responsible Investing (BRI) strategies for his clients.

Lucien is the President and Chief Compliance Officer for *Stephenson & Company* (go to www.stephensoncompany.com) where he is responsible for the firm's strategic vision and clarity when placing investment assets. He has been active in the financial industry for 18 years.

Lucien has a *Six Sigma Green Belt* from Villanova University and has an *Executive Certificate in Financial Planning* from The Ohio State University Max M. Fisher College of Business. Lucien is a proud member of *Kingdom Advisors* (go to www.Kingdomadvisors.org) and is *a Certified Kingdom Advisor*™. Lucien is also a Certified StratOp Facilitator for Marketplace & Churches by the Paterson Center, LLC.

Lucien is proud to subscribe to the *"Investing with Clarity*™*"* philosophy in relationship with money manager *Nepsis Capital Management*™ (go to www.nepsiscapital.com).

About the Company

AT STEPHENSON, YOU ARE WORKING with highly specialized investment professionals. Stephenson & Company is a full service fee-only Registered Investment Advisor (RIA) and financial planning firm based in Dover Ohio. We assist clients throughout the United States, the Caribbean and the world who want objectivity without any product/sales influence. Wealth accumulation and estate preservation includes coordinating our planning with tax, legal and insurance professionals. We follow a disciplined, clearly defined approach to balancing risk and return, and believe that educating clients enables them to make more knowledgeable decisions.

We offer the following comprehensive services to private individuals and small businesses:

- Portfolio analysis
- Asset allocation design
- Investment management
- Non-traditional college funding strategies
- Non-traditional retirement planning
- Estate planning
- Business Valuation
- Strategic and Operational Planning

When you, our client, are not willing or able to do analyses, our professional money managers take care of picking the companies best suited for your goals.

Stephenson and Company performs strategic and operational planning as well as business valuation services for small businesses. One of the things that we look at is measures of productivity, just as the portfolio manager would do. For us, it is all about how to create financial value for your company.

Acknowledgements

❧

I WOULD LIKE TO THANK my beloved wife, Chinyere, who personifies faithfulness. Her love and devotion to me have been my greatest earthly delight since the day I first caught sight of her at Kent State University in 1993.

To Adora and Kelechi, my amazing children – let your Light shine ever bright as you reach out and grab your life's potential!

I also had the help of others in producing this book:

Thanks to Tamma Ford, my editor, for her work in pulling this content together. Thanks to Primie Villa Parcon, for all the book's JPEGs and her interior illustrations. I am also grateful to Chuck D. Etzweiler, CFP, MBA, CIMA, CMT for his encouragements and the insights he so freely shared with me in our conversations about this topic.

Foreward by Mark Pearson

❧

IT'S ALL ABOUT CLARITY™. TODAY, more than ever, the ability for investors to know what investments they own and the ability to understand why they own them is paramount to being a successful investor. It's an idea that has got lost in the noise and confusion of the overabundance of media coverage surrounding the financial markets. *Total Clarity* is an inspiring look at the importance of clarity on the investment process… one that will help readers gain perspective on this critical information.

As the creator of the Four Key Components to Successful Investing™, I have had the opportunity to work closely with Lucien in promoting the idea of Investing with Clarity™. During this time, it is clear that he has both a passion for and a true understanding of the power of "Investing with Clarity™" as he has guided investors through the process of understanding the power of knowing what you own and why you own it.

Lucien, like me, believes the key to successful investing lies in having a clear investment *Philosophy, Strategy, Flexibility* and

Transparency. When any one of these "Four Keys" is missing, investors increase the risk to their investment success. Like a ship without a rudder, a lack of clarity renders investors powerless to navigate the sea of investment options and make the most of their investment opportunities. *Total Clarity* will help investors reclaim their rightful position as a captain of their own destiny in the investment process.

Investing is a complicated process for most investors. After all, look at the marketplace for today's investment products. Many firms now market in a manner that aims to convince investors to rely solely on computer-based algorithms. Often times, investors have no idea how these algorithms work, but feel they have no other choice but to trust in them with their hard-earned money and therefore their ability to realize their dreams.

The fact of the matter is that investing is both empirical and behavioral in nature. Investment success requires Clarity in the who, what, where, when, why and how of the process. The problem most investors face is the inability to know which investments they truly own and why they own them in the first place.

Through *Total Clarity*, Lucien also helps investors remember how essential Volatility is to the investment process. To most investors, Volatility is now considered "risk" and they have been trained to fear Volatility, while the fact of the matter still remains, Volatility is mandatory and needed for investors to be successful long-term. *Total Clarity* helps set the record straight on the importance of Volatility and its role in the investment process.

Unfortunately, many investors also do not have the Flexibility or Transparency needed in their investment approach to take advantage of the opportunities the marketplace creates for them to be successful investors long-term.

Whether a business owner knows it or not, they use the "four keys" as a function of running their business. A business owner will more than likely know what their investment philosophy and strategy is for the growth of their enterprise. Additionally, they will have flexibility in running their business and the transparency to assist in making business decisions. Lucien explores the importance of viewing your investments as a business owner would view the investments they had made in their own business. Understanding the reasons for making the investments in the first place and sticking to knitting during challenging times.

Whether you are new to investing or an experienced investor, I believe this book will provide you with insight and a framework to Investing with Clarity™ and therefore help you become a more successful investor over time.

That is *"Investing with Clarity."*

I applaud Lucien for sharing these insights with the public and hope the readers begin to embrace the idea of *Investing with Clarity*™.

Mark Pearson

Founder, President, Chief Investment Officer of *Nepsis Capital Management*™

November 2015

Author's Preface

❧

LET'S FACE IT – INVESTING is a complicated process for most investors. I mean after all, look at the marketplace for investment products. The industry is now at the point of trying to market, and convince investors to rely on, computer-based "algorithms" – when investors have no idea how they work. But they are still being expected to entrust their future profits to them!

The fact of the matter is that investing is both empirical and behavioral in nature. Investment success requires **Clarity** in the *who, what, where, when, why* and *how* of investing.

The problem most investors face is the inability to think with **Clarity** about the investments they own or why they own them in the first place.

To many uninformed investors, volatility is considered risky and they *fear* it. In spite of the fear, volatility is an advantage and helps grow profits – that is, if investors really wish to be successful over a *long-term period*.

Unfortunately, many investors do not have the **Flexibility** or choose advisors who have it, nor **Transparency** in the information they get to see or take advantage of the opportunities the marketplace creates for them to be successful investors long-term.

Clarity – The ability to know what investments you own; the ability to understand why you own them in the first place. That is investing in a nutshell.

I believe the key to successful investing must lie in what I refer to as the, "Four Key Components to Successful Investing." Those four keys include your **Investment Philosophy,** your **Strategy,** along with **Flexibility** and **Transparency**. When you are missing even one of the "Four Keys", you increase your risk beyond what is necessary – and lose out on potential profits that mean much more money for you in the long run.

A business owner intuitively knows that the "Four Keys" are a function of running his business, too. A business owner will more than likely know what his **Philosophy** and **Strategy** (a mission statement, a business plan, processes and procedures) are for the growth of the enterprise. Additionally, he will have **Flexibility** in running his business (decision-making, changes in direction, and so on) and the **Transparency** (enough facts and real data) to assist in making business decisions.

That approach helps a business owner to "invest time and energy with clarity in his business", just as it helps any investor build and manage a profitable portfolio with success.

Introduction

❧

"An investment operation is one which,
upon thorough analysis, promises safety of
principal and an adequate return.
Operations not meeting these
requirements are speculative."

~Benjamin Graham, from *'The Intelligent Investor'*

ARE YOU CERTAIN THAT YOU can sum up the four keys to *your own* investing? Does it resemble this set of keys:

1. A back-to-basics *philosophy* centered on clarity that has the validation of long-term success.
2. An investment *strategy* that takes advantage of market volatility, SCA™ (strategic cost averaging) and long-term investments in quality companies found in a select few sectors.
3. The *flexibility* needed to allow for seizing opportunities as they arise, a tax efficient management of a portfolio, as well as turning market volatility into an ally that gives higher returns over the long run.
4. A level of *transparency* that will guide your investment decisions by giving you facts about what you own and why you own it.

If it does not, I'll help you learn how to know what you own and – most especially – why you own it.

If everything you thought to be true about investing turned out to be false, when would you want to know it? Right away, of course!

As Warren Buffett (and many other wise men) has said, "Investing should be simple, but not easy." That is to say, it should be simple enough to understand how investing effectively works. It is this:

An investor buys a stock for less than its intrinsic value (that is, less than the generally agreed value of the company) and then sells when the stock or company is trading above its fair market value. [i] Easy, right? If it were that easy, there would be no need for this book!

BUY LOW; SELL HIGH

The ideas in this book *should not* be new to you. However, surprisingly enough, the ideas in this book will seem new to most readers. That is because the majority of investors have never been face-to-face with a true investment professional or, what is more, an investment professional with a philosophy and strategy for managing assets.

Today there are still very few barriers to entry in terms of presenting yourself as a financial advisor or money manager to any potential client. And that has been a real problem for investors … whether they know it or not.

A few individuals will still tell me with pride that they are with a *big wire house investment firm* 'X.' (These are the nation-wide firms with multiple branches.) But those who are honest oftentimes express disappointment with the level of service that they are receiving there, as well as the performance of the portfolio created for or *imposed* upon them. Many also find out too late that their CPA, who should be one of their most trusted advisors, is not an investment professional! In fact, all your CPA should do for you is *refer you to* a qualified investment professional. It is only a matter of time before investors realize that their financial professional knows even less about investing than they do, and will then seek out a new, true investment professional to manage their portfolios.

This book was written to inform the reader of the notion that the investor must have a constant adherence to certain fundamentals of owning a suitable, profitable, long-term portfolio of businesses. Most important is to have a clear ***investment philosophy, strategy and flexibility***^{TM}. Just as important, you the investor need to associate yourself with a portfolio manager who provides ***transparency*** in all things regarding your portfolio – you need facts, not opinions.

Since the dawn of the modern-day markets, investors have been trying to beat the odds. There have been many theorists and practitioners who have believed they have found the answer on how to achieve that.

The simple truth, however, is that the market is such a complex and volatile system that no investor is capable of beating it entirely. On the other hand, investing is a kind of game – one where you cannot lose in the end, so long as you play *only by the rules* that put the odds squarely in your favor. [ii]My goal is to give you those rules, as best I can.

There are indeed a number of principles that have proven historically to be effective at guiding successful investment decisions. As with all investments, there is *never* a 100 percent guarantee of success, but investing is all about hedging your bets. This is why I am going to provide the Total Clarity^{TM} every investor needs for successful investing.

VOLATILITY
Volatility is a term you hear if you pay attention to the investment markets. It is important to get volatility on your side. Volatility, very simply stated, is the fact that *stocks* go up in price and *stocks* go down in price. The higher the rise or the lower the drop

means the stock has more volatility. Yes, some stocks have prices that don't seem to change much, month after month or even year after year – we say that they have no volatility to speak of.

Additional to individual stock volatility, the market itself – whether the Dow Jones, the NASDAQ, the S&P 500, or any of the other world markets – can and does show overall volatility. Observers are used to these up and down movements and will always try to predict them. Don't listen to forecasters! Instead, just have a sound, well understood strategy that allows you to *take advantage of this volatility*. Yes, you can take advantage of it in ways we will see – and that can give your portfolio higher returns.

Here are just 2 recent historic examples of those upward and downward movements in the overall market to illustrate volatility a bit better to you:

- The Dow hit its all-time high on October 9, 2007, closing at **14,164**; less than 18 months later, it had fallen more than 50% to **6,594** (March 5, 2009). Volatility.
- In 1987, the Dow Jones plunged 23 percent in what remains the largest one-day loss in U.S. stock market history. It closed at **1,833**. Today, the Dow is in the mid-**17,000s** – far above the 2007 "all-time high"! Volatility.

Benjamin Graham, in his book "*The Intelligent Investor*", said this, and it demonstrates how you can be advantaged by volatility:

"Basically, price fluctuations have only one significant meaning for the true investor. *They provide him with an opportunity to buy wisely when prices fall sharply and to sell wisely when they advance a great deal.* At other times, he will do better if he forgets about the stock market and pays attention to his dividend returns and to the operating results of his companies. On the other hand, investing is a unique kind of casino – one where you cannot lose in the end, so long as you play only by the rules that put the odds squarely in your favor."

Total Clarity™ will help guide you through the volatility of the markets; you will learn to keep volatility in your corner – and understand *why* you should do so. After reading this book, you will have a clear understanding of how the volatility of your portfolio and of the greater market creates opportunities that allow you to profit. You will be owning great companies over time – and volatility is your friend on your way to investing profitably in this way.

Volatility is a critical component of successful long-term investment. First, the stock market indexes never go straight up. Or straight down. Never.

Thinking in terms of a 12-month return on investment is, I believe, a trap. The market certainly doesn't operate or think of its performance in 12-month increments. As history often shows, stock market indices and great businesses do not see their prices go straight up (or down), obviously for a variety of reasons. Investors fall into that trap when they think about how their portfolio performs. They too often look at weekly, monthly, quarterly or even annual returns as somehow important. They are not.

Regardless of the short-term performance of your portfolio, are you ready to sell the investments you own simply because there's volatility or a decline in the value of your portfolio? It is like asking if you are going to get off in the middle of your flight from St. Thomas to Atlanta just because there in some turbulence in the air! Why would you sell a great company or business that you own simply because it declined in value *in the short-term?*

Understanding volatility, and using it without emotion, is a critical component for the success of any long-term investor's portfolio, and that creates flexibility for you. It allows you to take advantage of the opportunities to buy more great companies when they become available at lower prices.

EMOTIONAL IQ – THE FEAR OR GREED CHOICE

I just spoke of emotions. Warren Buffet and all the smart long-term investors have had something to say about the emotions and reactivities stemming from people's greed and fear in the markets. In our approach, we take the sting out of these 2 core feelings that the markets seem to stir up.

Having a high or even an above-average Emotional IQ is very important as volatility increases in the market. Why? Because each investor has the tendency to start worrying more about how safe his investment really is (fear gets stirred up), or wondering how severe the stock market correction will be in the future (and start to feel greedy if it seems in his favor). By the way, a *market correction*, very simply stated, means that the overall market moves towards "fair value pricing" to correct a trend that created too high or too low prices overall. In other words, the Dow Jones Industrial Average (or other index) will move up or move down. Some analysts don't call it a correction – either up or down – until there is at least a 10 percent pricing difference. Market corrections, and the associated turbulence, are a prime source of greed and fear!

When you fly from JFK to St. Thomas, more than likely you will encounter turbulence along the way. The pilot of the aircraft does not, however, make the decision to turn back and return to JFK because of a little bit of turbulence. People wouldn't travel anymore if they were always concerned about turbulence! In the environment in which the aircraft operates, you naturally get occasional turbulence. A bit of turbulence is a natural part of the trading and investing environment, too … and no one would trade in the markets without it! You can use the volatility and market corrections to your advantage – doing just as the best and most profitable long-term investors do.

Your Investment Philosophy

❧

THE FIRST OF YOUR FOUR steps for successful investing? A back-to-basics *philosophy* centered on clarity that has been validated for your *long-term success*. Let's see how that works as we examine:

- Having too many baskets of eggs and appropriate diversification
- Buying stocks, funds or indices versus buying *companies*
- Buying low and selling high (most don't!)
- Research what you will own; watch for and use volatility as a tool for profitability and risk management
- Two interesting investment instruments that are not for everyone

The first step in my own investment process with any new client starts with the foundation, we start with an "Investment Policy Statement" or IPS. This is where we seek to understand your goals, needs and wants. The purpose of this *Investment Policy Statement* ("IPS") is really to create clear understanding between myself and the portfolio manager and the investor about *why you are investing*. What are your financial goals? This is all about developing your philosophy around the achievement of those personal goals.

DIVERSIFICATION

None of us should "put all our eggs in one basket," because if the basket falls to the ground, the likelihood of all the eggs cracking is high. What lies at the heart of almost every investor's philosophy and strategy is the principle of diversification. Or – several baskets of eggs, rather than just one.

This idea really took root in 1990 with investors, when Harry Markowitz and William Sharpe were awarded the Nobel Prize in Economics for their work on *Modern Portfolio Theory (MPT)*. The main premise of MPT was the concept of portfolio diversification and spreading one's risk in different directions to reduce the investor's *variability* of returns. (I refer to it here as "volatility"). This spreading of risk is similar with what the insurance industry has done for centuries.

This book is not a critique of MPT per se, but a review of how I believe it has been used out of context for many years. For example, many in the investment world recommend diversification to reduce risk as the best way of being a careful investor (by not putting all of your eggs into one basket).

I say investors put their eggs in *too many* baskets, and thus fall into the perils of over diversification. Investors have been so oversold on diversification that their fear of having too many eggs in one basket has caused them to put far too little cash into companies they know thoroughly, and far too much in others which they know nothing about.

We've all heard 'industry experts' expound on the benefits of diversification (to spread and thus reduce your risk of losses), and I agree with the general concept, as a stock portfolio must be diversified to some degree.

From an investment point of view, if you own many stocks in a single sector, and that sector suddenly drops in value, you can lose a substantial amount of your principal. But can you go too far in spreading your risk? I believe that you indeed can.

The majority of my investment clients built their personal wealth with significant stock ownership in one business, and a very small minority built their wealth with a portfolio of multiple businesses. There is an ancient proverb that states each person should diversify his income source into *multiple and unrelated* forms of business – one never knows where disaster will strike, or how.

There are many studies demonstrating why diversification works. The concept is supported by the premise of combining assets with different properties that have little correlation to each other, and one ends up reducing price volatility. The purpose of diversification is to reduce unsystematic risk (the risk associated with a single industry, sector or security) within a portfolio. An inverse relationship has always existed between the amounts of unsystematic risk within a portfolio and what can be diversified. Unsystematic risks are diversifiable risks, as they are not tied to the market as a whole but, rather, are unique to a specific industry, business, or security.

A properly diversified portfolio should be invested in assets of multiple asset types, including emerging markets, international, mid-cap (companies with a market capitalization of $2-$10 billion), and large cap companies (companies with a market capitalization of more than $10 billion). Invest not just in the US, but in strong overseas markets, too, in other words – if you can, and if this fits your goals.

Think about this: Does a successful business just invest in one product? A one-product business may just go out of business when the consumers no longer want their only product!

INDIVIDUAL STOCKS OR FUNDS?
These comments go to understanding what you own.

After reading Philip Fisher, the author of the book "*Uncommon Stocks and Uncommon Profits*", you will realize that you do not need to own an S&P 500 Index Exchange Traded Fund (ETF), a mutual fund with 250 positions, or even a stock and bond portfolio with over 100 positions. For instance, Warren Buffett's mega-wealthy and very stable company Berkshire Hathaway owns only 45 stocks, and focuses primarily on just 15 (having a very large number of shares in these 15).

I believe investors do not understand the structure of indexes that they use as benchmarks for the performance of their own portfolios. This is very evident based on the performance of the S&P 500 over the last five years or so, and the variables that contributed to its performance.

The media and some of the so-called experts on television often talk about how investors should just invest in the S&P 500 Index Funds, since most money managers don't outperform that Index anyway. I believe it is ridiculous for an investor to think that she should put all of her money into one index. Many investors do not even understand how these indexes are calculated, or where the returns of these indices come from (that is, which component stocks are having stellar performances, as opposed to others which are declining miserably).

It is virtually impossible to research, *understand* and be in agreement to own all the companies that compose any one index. That is why I always advise to buy individual companies (they are easy to research and get information about), not indexes of companies that remain quite obscure to most investors. When you selectively choose your companies for your portfolio, you know what you have – and why.

Do indexes have perhaps a place in your portfolio? Yes, but that depends on your goals! In short, talking to your advisor about your goals will start to bring clarity about the type of investment vehicles you need in your portfolio. Goals first, understanding what you own next, then you hold onto that portfolio to help you achieve your goals.

Buy Low and Sell High

Is that really what you are doing – buying as cheaply as you can and selling as high as possible? Let's see how that works for the vast majority of investors.

Many investors may remember the late 1990s when the S&P 500 was performing better than many investors were accustomed to – better than many other indexes and similar portfolios. That led to many investors investing in that index at the peak of that great performance. And they all remember what happened shortly after that – the S&P 500 went on for the next decade to underperform (i.e.: go down in value). Many investors became frustrated and disenfranchised with investing in the stock market as a whole; as a result, many just cashed out.

Here's the rub: Those investors that bought at the peak *bought high* and very likely all cashed out by *selling low*! No, no – you must buy low and sell high, remember?

I express to my clients how important it is to be a long-term investor in well-chosen *businesses*, as opposed being a speculator jumping on every movement in the stock market.

Many investors become frustrated and disenfranchised with investing in the stock market as a whole after experiences like this, because they listened to the talking heads on television – most of whom have no experience or qualifications to be talking about business or investments – and jumped on the bandwagon. There may be only one gentleman on television who is actually qualified to talk about investments, he wears a bowtie and comes on at 5 a.m. on one of the financial networks.

I was reading an article by James Altucher, "*The Ultimate Cheat Sheet for What You Should Do With All Of Your Money.*"[iii] He said that he once accidentally got an email that was intended for a famous well-known investor. It was from his broker and the email contained his portfolio. Altucher can't say how this accident happened, but it did. He said, "Of course I opened the email."

It turned out that this investor was a man who writes about lots of *stocks*, but his entire portfolio was in *municipal bonds*!

That's why I say don't waste time listening to the talking heads on TV. They are primarily there for entertainment.

We've known since the 1970s, since the publication of Hyman Minsky's book, "*Stabilizing Unstable Economy*", that volatility is a good thing; that "stability is destabilizing"; that any relative tranquility encourages more risk-taking.

In other words, if there was no volatility in the stock market, entrepreneurs and investors alike would do nothing else in the economy but stay at home at their computers and buy stocks, leaving the rest of the economy to simply collapse.

STOCKS OR COMPANIES?

NOTE: I don't like to call them 'stocks' or 'equities' (these are the same thing by two names), but instead I help my client to understand that we're buying companies. We are buying real, functioning businesses. We are becoming business owners when we purchase shares of a company – we have become one of that company's shareholders (which is another word for 'partial owner'; you own a small 'share' of the business).

A significant part of working with clients is leading them to think differently about equity or stock market investments. As I mentioned in the opening of this book, the most significant and profound idea I teach is the notion that you must have a constant adherence to certain fundamental components to a successful portfolio. That is, having a clear philosophy, strategy and flexibility, and hiring a portfolio manager who provides transparency regarding your portfolio.

I teach my clients that we are not buying into the *stock* market and we not buying *stocks*. We are buying great companies. You must understand that, as Philip Fisher says, "The successful investor is usually an individual who is inherently interested in business problems". The stock market has always been and still is the most efficient tool available for buying great companies we want to own for the long-term. My core belief is that you all should know what companies you own in your portfolio, why you own that particular company, and how much that particular company costs. I help my clients find a portfolio manager such as *Nepsis Capital Management*™ with a research team to identify quality, undervalued companies. The researchers' job is to do in-depth research and analysis of that company. Let's look at the two basic ways that any investor researches a company. The first is called 'technical' and the second 'fundamental' analysis.

TECHNICAL ANALYSIS

Technical analysis looks at the numbers – ratios, statistics, following charts with ideas like the 30-day moving average trend line and so on. You need technology to do this type of analysis.

For its adherents, there is a large market for selling software and hardware to individuals who seem to have lots of spare time to gaze at technical charting and chart formations like 'inverse saucers' or the 'double bottoms.'

Technical analysis gives an hour-by-hour set of data if that is what interests you. However, I believe investors are better off taking a long-term view, by holding investments in individual companies over extended periods of time.

In fact, after reading Michael Lewis's book, "*Flash Boys: A Wall Street Revolt*"[iv] which is about how so-called high frequency traders (HFT – the "flash boys") are gaming the market, you realize that there are only two types of people who make money buying stocks. The first type is those people who hold stocks *FOREVER* – like Warren Buffett, who some have said has never sold a share of Berkshire Hathaway since 1967, or Bill Gates, who for 20 years has basically held onto his original Microsoft stock. And then there is the second type: the people who hold stocks for a millionth of a second, as described in "Flash Boys".

The flash boys were taking advantage, starting in 2009, of a costly and brand-new technical-analysis technology aimed at just their own industry. Unless you are going to pay the $10 million it takes for a five-year lease to access this "flash-trading" line, you cannot trade like the stock market players who buy access to the line. In fact, if we were able to pay for access to this line, we'd have to sign an agreement that prohibits anyone who leased the line from allowing others to use it! Any big bank with such a lease on that line could use it for "its own proprietary trading, but was forbidden from sharing it with its brokerage customers." We wonder why the flash boys have not yet had their tactics outlawed. This is the next thing to illegal and I don't recommend you try anything approaching this! In my view, a little technical analysis can go a long way – just don't get hooked into reading charts every day! Long-term investors don't need to.

FUNDAMENTAL ANALYSIS

If someone asked me what I believe to be the best process for picking great companies to invest in over the long-term would be from an academic viewpoint, I would say fundamental analysis. In fact, contrary to a lot of technical analysis tools, it is the only approach fully available to the average or retail investor.

Contrary to technical analysis, this fundamental research is often totally free of cost. You can look at financial reports of each company of interest – as the publication of these reports is an obligation when a company is listed for trade, you have access to them. Is it profitable? How much debt does it have? Does gross sales revenue seem to be growing? What is the trading history (volume, price, etc.)? Then non-numeric fundamental analysis can take place. What exactly does the company sell and do I understand what it is? Has the company got a steady management team or is it in flux? Are they staying true to past partnership agreements or not? Are they developing new partnerships, new markets, new products? Here you look for the answers to your questions as if you were going to buy the entire company – become its owner. What is it you'd really like to know?

I know that one selection process that has provided the greatest amount of wealth has been this process of investing in a business as though you are the owner of that business. Just as a business person looks at some basic abilities of a company before investing in it for the first time (think about how Angel Investors or Venture Capitalists choose the businesses they will invest in), a business owner also strategically re-invests in his company over time.

I, and our own portfolio managers, believe in the same selection process. This coincides with Philip Fisher's statement, "The successful investor is usually an individual who is inherently interested in business problems."

Fisher achieved an excellent record during his 70-plus years of money management by investing in well managed, high-quality growth companies, which he held for the long term. For example, he bought Motorola stock in 1955 and didn't sell it until his death in 2004.[v]

This fundamental analysis is a look at individual stocks as *companies* – as commercial enterprises operating in a real marketplace. Fundamental analysis is based on a system of facts about a company that help in determining the fair market value – a dollar value – of it. The value you arrive at is then compared to the current market price to determine whether to buy, sell or hold that company in your portfolio.

Fundamental analysis, then, is really looking at the right data to answer the questions: "How well is this company doing? How strong, effective and profitable is it compared to companies in the same industry?" It is a look at a list of measurements – not all of them numeric, but about the business "basics" or foundational issues. This analysis will tell you all about a company's strength in its own marketplace.

As far as fundamental analysis is concerned, I believe in something called a 'bottom-up' analysis, where we analyze the specific company, followed by an analysis of its industry, then looking at the greater economy in which it operates.

When we look at the individual *company* first, we find out things like its liquidity, sales activity, profitability, and debt ratios. These are all basics to consider when looking at the *company* in terms of fundamental analysis.

Then a look at its *industry* is vital, to find out the current strength of the overall industry in the larger economy, whether it is going through a smooth growth time or a rough reorganization, perhaps due to some new technological advancement, and so on.

We follow up with a review of the overall economic environment of the country, because it does affect the ability of industries and companies to operate; this includes how the stock market is doing, and what the movements (or lack thereof) are as regard monetary policy, fiscal policy, interest rates, business cycles and even cross-industry trends.

The most widely used approach, though, when it comes to fundamental analysis is the top-down approach. The above approach started at the narrow end of a funnel, as it were – this approach starts at the wide mouth of the funnel, and works its way down. It analyzes, so as to identify a good stock for purchase by the investor: the economy, the specific industry, then specific companies in an industry.[vi]

Of these 2 versions of fundamental analysis, I prefer the bottom-up approach. It de-emphasizes the significance of

economic and market cycles and focuses on the analysis of individual stocks or individual companies. When you use a bottom-up analytical approach, you concentrate your attention on
a specific company rather than on the industry in which that
company operates or on the economy as a whole. When taking a bottom-up approach, it is possible to detect one or more
individual companies that may do well even if their respective
industries are not performing very well.

Decision-making based on a bottom-up investing strategy
naturally entails doing a thorough review of the company in
question, but – as I said above – there is plenty of publicly ac-
cessible information to help you do this. Your analytical job
includes becoming familiar with the company's products and
services; using available financial reports and stability research
reports; it includes reading press reports about change in management team members and about new product releases or new
sales partnerships and so on.

This Fundamental Analysis approach, in my opinion, gives
you, the long-term company investor, a better potential outcome
and you become an investor in a sound business that you now
understand fairly well. This fundamental approach also tells
you when a company does not have the basic foundations for
success, and you can let that poor choice go. You simply move on
to the analysis of the next company on your list.

WHEN TO ADJUST YOUR PORTFOLIO

Carefully select companies you understand with a diversified
portfolio in mind; adjust its contents accordingly as opportunities
come forth and present themselves. How, though, if you are in
these companies for the long haul? Two primary ways: Watch for
new *opportunities* outside your current holdings; watch for *volatility*
that is to your advantage as you build up your current holdings!

Here is an example of the first way: A portfolio manager that my firm had developed a relationship with continually invested between 20 percent and 30 percent of my clients' portfolios in emerging (new) and international market companies, according to his analysis of what was happening in those parts of the world. I am continually pleased with the companies purchased for my clients. He seizes opportunities of value. That is one way of adjusting for growth and profits.

Here is an example of the second way: The price of one of your favored companies dips significantly. You already have some of its stock. This is when you use your available cash to buy more of this company at the lower price (as I have demonstrated elsewhere in these pages). You should always keep a certain amount of cash in the portfolio (or other account) to take advantage of individual share price volatility and that elusive stock market correction. That is another way to readjust your portfolio.

Selling is not on the table for readjustments! When an investor finally understands that he owns businesses, he doesn't sell the investments at inappropriate times. He instead invests like a business owner, not a day or flash trader. He is investing with Total Clarity™. Philip Fisher, the author of the book "*Common Stocks and Uncommon Profits*", said, "If the job has been correctly done when a common stock is purchased, the time to sell it is almost never." But, as shown above, you can add to your holding when volatility plays a lower purchase price into your hand.

When investing and thinking like a business owner who does not sell his business in anticipation (fear) of a recession, but doubles down on advertising and networking for new clients and so on for continuity of operations, you also will want to continuously re-invest in your businesses (your shares).

Be far less concerned about what the markets will do over a short period and far more concerned about the ability of the companies you own to carry out their own business plan or strategy.

You must understand that stock market corrections will come and go. Make no mistake about it. The media loves to focus on corrections and what's happening in the stock market; that 'drama' is what sells advertising and stimulates viewer emotion. The media is only there to force you to make emotional decisions. Just be aware that the media is simply there for entertainment purposes and, of course, to sell the products of its advertisers. That's it. Very few financial news commentators are market or investment professionals.

I just need you to understand that the US markets remain "fairly" valued. And I believe that there are always great opportunities in certain situations in emerging markets and all over Europe. I allow my clients to take advantage of those opportunities as they arise or reveal themselves.

Remember that Emotional IQ is as important in investing as in life and business. Let other investors allow their emotions to create opportunities for you to continue to investing for the long-term in some tremendous businesses. Dr. Jeremy Siegel of the Wharton School of Business, in his book, "*Stocks for the Long Run 5/E: The Definitive Guide to Financial Market Returns & Long-Term Investment Strategies*", stated clearly that the longer you own stocks, the less risky they become. He also went on to say, "History convincingly demonstrates that stocks have been and will remain the best investment for all those seeking long-term gains."

I continually tell my clients to expect that elusive 20 percent market correction, first because <u>it is coming</u>, and second that it is simply <u>an opportunity</u> to add to your current positions in great businesses. Remember, "When investors are fearful, you must become greedy," according to Warren Buffett. Buffett also stated, "Look at market fluctuations as your friend rather than your enemy; profit from folly; do not to anticipate in it." In other words, others get frightened by a price drop, they panic and sell. You, on the other hand, get 'greedy' in the sense you use that lower price to acquire more of the stocks you already own, cheaply.

No one knows when the next big stock market correction is going to happen. Therefore, why worry about a correction if you know that you own great businesses and have a solid investment philosophy and strategy? You understand that your portfolio manager has great flexibility and transparency to guide you through your investment process. So, why worry about a correction?

If you were investing in Greece in 2015, you could having been facing all four types of unsystematic risk (depending on the type of assets you were invested in): Business risk; financial risk; default risk and political risk! Yikes!

That said, it is important to remember that no matter how well diversified your portfolio may be, a certain amount of risk will always be present. You can reduce a risk associated with individual stocks called non-systematic risk, but there are inherent market risks called systematic risks that affect nearly every stock.

It is a fundamental idea in investing that no amount of diversification can prevent systematic risk. Systematic risk is simply the risk associated with the entire market. In order to be a successful long-term investor, one must embrace systematic risk and volatility, realizing that volatility is a beneficial component of investing, not a disadvantage. In fact, I will do my best to prove to you that volatility is your friend and one of the most important tools you have as an investor. You must grasp the concept that volatility creates the opportunity for an investor to continue to invest in great companies at lower prices.

MORE ON VOLATILITY AND RISK

This is for those of you interested in more technical detail.

There is a scientific formula that measures risk or volatility called *beta*. Beta, a word that every investor must know, is a measure of *volatility* of an asset's return *in relation to the overall market*. Risk is just volatility relative to that of the market. **An investor must have volatility (or risk) to make money in the market.** Bonds, or any fixed income portion of your portfolio, are only "beta reducers" – aids in reducing the overall volatility of your portfolio.

If you are retired, have less than five years until retirement or if you simply need to draw assets from your portfolio, then a portion of your portfolio – say up to 50 percent of it – would be in fixed income. There are times, especially when interest rates are low and the Federal Reserve Bank continues to talk about raising interest rates, that you do not want to own fixed income in your portfolio. You want to own investments like *Real Estate Investment Trusts* (REITs), which are sold as stocks, or utility stocks – not fixed income instruments.

You see, as interest rates rise, the price of your bonds is guaranteed to fall. Thus, if I have 10 years or more until I need to draw cash from my portfolio, then 100 percent of my portfolio would be in individual equities (stocks). 100 percent of my holdings would be in *companies*. The cash or fixed income portion of my portfolio would be in the form of a cash value dividend-paying whole life insurance policy. See "*Becoming Your Own Banker*" by R. Nelson Nash.

Both "systematic risk" and "undiversifiable risk" connote the same thing and in this book, they both may be used interchangeably. However, my philosophy is also based on the idea that many investors do not like volatility, because they do not have the flexibility to take advantage of volatility. It is worth repeating that the greatest investor in the world from a human standpoint, Mr. Buffett, said, "Look at market fluctuations as your friend rather than your enemy; profit from folly rather than participate in it."

Additionally, investors have no clarity, or very little. They do not understand what they presently own, and as a result, lack the means to have the conviction to continually invest in great companies over time.

So, how many stocks in a portfolio are needed for it to be considered truly "diversified?"

As the number of stocks increases, the level of unsystematic risk declines. However, there is a point of diminishing returns with regard to adding securities to a portfolio. In Edwin J. Elton and Martin J. Gruber's book "*MPT and Investment Analysis*", they conclude that the average standard deviation (market risk) of a portfolio of one stock was 49.2 percent. Furthermore, they found that methodically increasing the number of stocks in the average well-balanced portfolio has the effect of reducing the portfolio's standard deviation (market risk) to 19.2 percent. Remarkably, they also found that with a portfolio of twenty stocks, the risk was reduced to about 20 percent. Therefore, increasing a portfolio from 20 stocks to 1,000 only reduced the portfolio risk by about 0.8 percent, while the first 20 stocks reduced the portfolio's risk by 29.2 percent (49.2 percent less 20 percent).[vii]

Many investors have the misguided view that risk is proportionately reduced with each new stock added to a portfolio, when in fact this couldn't be further from the truth.

There is strong evidence that you can only reduce your risk so much, at which point there is no additional benefit from diversification. However, the previously mentioned study is not suggesting that buying just any twenty stocks equates with optimum diversification!

One achieves true diversification when one combines assets with unlike properties (low correlation) to achieve optimal efficiency. In other words, diversification only works because different asset classes within a portfolio are usually not perfectly correlated. Thus, a 20-35 stock portfolio should include stocks from amongst various sectors and industries to ensure that variation in returns is being reduced.

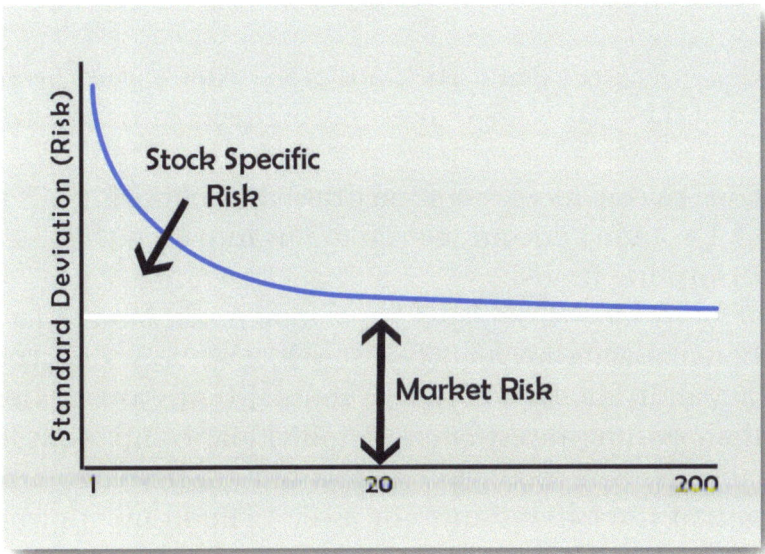

Mutual Funds

❧

I THINK A WORD ABOUT mutual funds is in order, given the pervasiveness of these 'packaged' investment vehicles in retail investors' portfolios.

I hope to convince you of the drawbacks of buying *any mutual fund*. I wouldn't encourage you to buy into even the so-called top-performing funds.

Let me restate this: ***Don't buy mutual funds!*** Do not let your portfolio manager buy any of these vehicles into your account.

Many individuals believe that mutual funds are a safer option than owning investments in individual companies. In my estimation, this is totally false. Most mutual funds do a pretty poor job of diversifying investor assets. The irony in owning a mutual fund is that it invests in several hundred companies, but without guarantees that you are *optimally* diversified.

Many mutual fund holders suffer not from being *under*diversified, but rather *over*diversified. Some funds, especially the larger ones, literally have to hold hundreds of stocks and consequently, its investors are likewise holding so many stocks that it is impossible for them to know at any given time what they actually own … much less what the returns on any component are. Not just too many eggs in one basket – but too many baskets of eggs!

To add fuel to the fire, many investors in pursuit of perceived diversification will end up owning ten or more stock funds that have over 200 holdings each. With 10 funds, one has over 2,000 stock holdings – certainly with a good deal of overlap and repetition and certainly with a huge number of underperforming components. This, coupled with a minuscule percentage of ownership per security, equates to a severely inefficient portfolio. The investor gets the double-whammy of being overdiversified and ineffective at the same time. This is why mutual fund investors tend to jump from one fund to another. A *Dalbar Study* concluded that investors in mutual funds earn substantially less than what the market can offer. In 2014, the average equity mutual fund investor underperformed the S&P 500 by a margin of 8.19 percent. The broader market return was more than double that of the average equity mutual fund investor's return (13.69 percent as versus 5.50 percent).

In 2014, the average fixed income mutual fund investor underperformed the *Barclays Aggregate Bond Index* by a margin of 4.81 percent. The broader bond market returned over five times that of the average fixed income mutual fund investor (5.97 percent as versus 1.16 percent).

In 2014, the 20-year annualized S&P return was 9.85 percent, while the 20-year annualized return for the average equity mutual fund investor was only 5.19 percent – a gap of 4.66 percent.

The Dalbar's *Quantitative Analysis of Investor Behavior*, which has measured investor behavior since 1994, has measured the effects of investor decisions to buy, sell and switch into and out of mutual funds over short- and long-term timeframes. The results consistently show that the *average investor earns less* – in many cases, much less – than mutual fund performance reports would suggest.

No matter what the state of the mutual fund industry, whether boom or bust: the *Dalbar Study* concludes that investment results are more dependent on <u>*investor behavior*</u> than on <u>*fund performance*</u>. Mutual fund investors who hold on to their investments have been more successful than those who try to time the market.

The greatest losses in investment portfolios occur after a market decline. This is because investors tend to sell after experiencing a paper loss and start investing only after the markets have recovered their value. There is fear and some panic! The devastating result of this behavior is being out of the market at the wrong time to take advantage of volatility purchases (as I demonstrate below). Once ultimate recovery and rise are reached, it is too late to benefit.

Someone said diversification is like a box of chocolates: It is good, but only in reasonable quantities. The common consensus is that a well-balanced portfolio with approximately twenty stocks diversifies away the maximum amount of market risk. Benjamin Graham in his classic book, *"The Intelligent Investor,"* declares that true diversification "can only be accomplished by a limited number of holdings, as owning additional stocks takes away the potential of big gainers significantly impacting your bottom-line. You have to know what you own, and why you own it." Graham's book should be on the shelf of every investor.[viii] In other words, owning too many stocks dilutes the return of the portfolio because your good performers get lost in the mass of negative-return or zero-return stocks.

Peter Lynch said, "Owning stocks is like having children you don't get involved with more than you can handle. The part-time stock picker probably has time to follow 8-12 companies, and to buy and sell shares as conditions warrant. There don't have to be more than five companies in the portfolio at any one time. My client portfolios typically own 25 to 35 high-quality companies which are ideal diversification without over diversification, and amounts over 40 companies do not provide any significant diversification benefits."[ix] Peter Lynch – successful for a long number of years in the markets for his clients; read everything you can that he has written!

It is the same case with large mutual funds investing in hundreds of stocks. For example, say you own shares in *Vanguard Total Stock Market Index Fund*. As of June 30, 2015, this fund had more than 3,814 separate holdings. (Nearly 4,000! Could you even inform yourself of that many companies?) Many of its top ten largest holdings like Apple, General Electric and Berkshire Hathaway are already well-diversified companies in their own right. In my opinion, it is impossible to achieve the true benefits by owning any of the funds' top ten holdings amongst the 3,814 other holdings in this single fund. According to Warren Buffett, "Wide diversification is only required when investors do not understand what they are doing." Understand what you are doing: The bottom-line is to understand your own philosophy and avoid following the crowd.[x]

401(K) ACCOUNTS

Here are some useful comments for those holding 401 (k) accounts (and to those business owners and executive committees of those companies offering this type of plan). Those accounts don't need to be 'sitting there' until your retirement. They have another useful function for you. Read on if these accounts are part of your portfolio – and especially if you are a business owner yourself.

Find out if your company allows "*in-service withdrawals*". Owners of the business can contact the third party administrator of the plan, to be certain that their 401(k) allows in-service withdrawals. If it doesn't have this option, ask the third party administrator to add "in-service withdrawal" language to their plan documents. Once the company allows in-service withdrawals on

401(k) assets, your retirement account can convert from mutual funds to individual company (stock) assets and other more productive instruments.

Once you initiate an in-service withdrawal from your 401(k), those assets must go into an Individual Retirement Arrangement (IRA); if not, you will pay a 10 percent penalty and income taxes if you are under age 59 ½. The next step would be to initiate a Rule 72 (t) Withdrawal, paying the income taxes while they are still employed.

There are three payments methods possible for accessing your IRA funds before age 59 ½ without penalty. You will use one of the three methods of distribution spelled out in section 72(t) of the Internal Revenue Code. The three methods are:

1. Life Expectancy
2. Amortization
3. Annuitizing

Let me review a couple methods for using this to your advantage. Please note that I am not offering tax advice, and you will need to confirm all of this information with your tax advisor before jumping in and using it.

EXAMPLE:
Say Brian, a 50-year-old business owner, is the owner of an IRA from which he would like to start taking distributions beginning in 2016. He would like to avoid the §72(t) additional 10% tax imposed on early distributions by taking advantage of the substantially-equal-periodic-payment exception. Brian's IRA account balance is $400,000 as of December 31, 2015 (the last valuation prior to the first distribution). 120% of the applicable federal mid-term rate is assumed to be 2.98%, and this will be

the interest rate Brian uses under the amortization and annuitizing methods. Brian will determine distributions over his own life expectancy only.

EXAMPLE:

A client who owns a business with a company 401K contacted his third party administrator (TPA) to change his company's plan documents to allow "in-service withdrawals". That means all of the employees in the company 401(k) could do an in-service withdrawal as well. Then he rolled his 401(k) assets into an IRA, where the money manager was Nepsis Capital Management. This client was so pleased with the enhancements to his portfolio, as a result he moved additional assets to the same money manager; at one point I had to urge him to stop telling referrals or his business colleagues all of his own personal and fabulous results. I wanted him to understand that his returns in one year was *not likely* to be the experience of new investors he evangelized. He just had perfect timing, as we bought into his portfolio after a market correction. In other words, his referrals' results may not be as good as his. The portfolio manager likes to focus on the process and not any individual results.

EXAMPLE:

A physician client rolled her 401k assets into an IRA managed by Nepsis Capital Management. She keeps the fixed income portion of her portfolio in the cash value of a Whole Life Insurance Policy. She periodically borrows from the cash value or uses the cash value as collateral for loans to purchase equipment for her business. She is employing the "infinite banking" concept found in the book *"Becoming Your Own Banker"* by R.

Nelson Nash. Please remember the primary reason to purchase a life insurance policy is to protect one's beneficiaries through the death benefit. However, permanent life insurance can also serve as an *accumulation tool* that has some very unique benefits (i.e.: the cash value may be protected from creditors, lawsuits and even divorce). To qualify for the life insurance, this client took a health examination to determine her insurability. Not everyone is insurable. The main way that a permanent life insurance policy is positioned to be tax advantaged is though policy loans. In retirement, she plans to take policy loans and never repay them. Policy loans may reduce the cash value and death benefit of a policy, and if they are not repaid, a loan could cause a policy to lapse. Remember she's going to be borrowing money from the life insurance company and using her cash value as collateral so there is no risk to the insurance company. These policies have some rules and usage regulations, so she informed herself – to best avoid taxation, penalties and so on. Some of her employees continue to contribute to the 401(k), but she does not offer a match to her staff (many companies do not). In making unlimited contributions to her life insurance policy and using it as a private bank, she has *unlimited borrowing power*. She is borrowing from the life insurance company and using her cash value as collateral. The strategy gives her "use and control" of her money instead of sticking money into the 401(k). Remember, money that you place inside your 401(k) is not tax-free – it is only tax-*deferred*. Meaning that you are deferring the tax payment, but also the tax calculation. When she pays off the loan to the life insurance company, she has that money to use again and again, in addition to the tax-free dividends she earned on her cash value that never left the policy. She has no intention of retiring anytime soon! Are there other insurance-based strategies that may work better for you? Perhaps, so talk to an educated investment advisor. For instance, instead of using margin to buy securities (never a good strategy, in my view), I have taught some of my clients to borrow from the life insurance company using a small percentage only of the cash value as collateral to purchase investments; that way there's less risk (the life insurance company has their cash value as collateral).

"I don't like using leverage or margin to make investments, but I have borrowed from my life insurance company using the cash value of my whole life insurance policy as collateral and I have made investments in companies that I like and want to hold onto for long time. Once I make a profit I pay the loan back immediately." Crystal Langdon of *Crystal Clear Finances* in Albany New York, and a CFP® certificant, says she does not recommend that her clients borrow more than 10% from the insurance company using their whole life policy as collateral in order make investments.

LESSONS LEARNED

Remember that the best strategies for selecting the stocks and investments are personalized to your circumstances. Don't jump into an investment vehicle without understanding its ramifications on your personal goals and needs!

You don't need a huge number of stocks in your portfolio – but you do need enough of them to provide adequate diversification. Buffett's Berkshire Hathaway owns only 45 stocks – and investing is their billion-dollar business!

Remember you are buying companies that you know something about. Do fundamental analysis.

With mutual funds – or worse, with several of them or other index instruments – in your portfolio, you cannot possibly know or research all the component companies. If you did, you would probably not want most of them! Likewise, a 401(k) account holds many companies or instruments you may not be aware of. Get informed.

Be in it for the long haul. How many ways can I say this?! Momentary shifts are for the flash boys and the day traders, not you. Hold firm.

This said, volatility, along with sound research into a company's fundamentals, are tools that help increase the value of your portfolio over the long term – and you are indeed aiming for long term success! Buy low – watch volatility so that when your stock's price drops a percentage or dollar amount that means you can buy more shares cheaply, do so!

THE BEST WORDS FOR LAST – "I DON'T KNOW"

You will read about it again in the next pages, but it bears much repetition. It should be part of your investment and research philosophy.

Here is the favorite phrase of all intelligent investors, the best investment advisors and the smartest portfolio managers that you may find yourself working with:

"I don't know."

Someone may ask me, "The market just took a dive, so it is bound to go back up in the next week or two – right?" My response must be, "I don't know."

If you see on television or read even in the best financial or investment newspapers that, "We predict that the market will rise 2,500 more points by year-end." … and you ask me if I believe that to be true, my response again must be, "I don't know."

If someone gives you a stock tip and tells you it's the next big Google or the next Microsoft, what do you say? "I don't know if that's true or not – let me do some fundamental research." And after that research, you still may not know!

"I don't know" needs to be your response, too – just as you should expect it to be the best response from your investment advisor or portfolio manager. Anyone who says he knows something for certain in these financial markets is kidding himself… and trying to kid you into investing your hard-earned money with him. Run the other way.

James Altucher, in one of his columns, professes to be able to write a history of all financial scams of the past 15 years, and here is the list he provided, without any descriptions, of course: "Reg S, Calendar Trading, Mutual Fund Timing, Death spirals, Front running, Pump and Dump, manipulating illiquid stocks, Ponzi schemes, insider information."[xi]

Likewise, if you come across any of those phrases, or just the whispered word "scam", or the whispered phrase, "It's too good to be true." … Run the other way! The big Wall Street boys have the ways and means to take advantage of the market in ways the retail investor cannot even guess. Yes, perhaps. You the retail or individual investor do not ever have the institutional investor's tools or advantages. So you have basically one recourse in order to make money in the financial markets. What's the only way shown over time to make money?

Buy quality stocks that you understand,
with excellent fundamentals,
and hold them forever!

We have looked a bit here at investment philosophy as well as why mutual funds should not be any part of your thinking. We have seen what we "do not know" – in fact, we know nothing! Nothing about the future of any industry, market or company, nor certain types of investment vehicles.

And this leads us to our Key #2, which is all about a portfolio strategy.

Your Investment Strategy

VOLATILITY AND RETURNS

YOU NEED AN INVESTMENT *STRATEGY* for your long-term investments in quality companies found in a select few sectors that
utilizes market volatility and Dollar-Cost-Averaging/Strategic
Cost Averaging (DCA/SCA™). Let's see how that strategy works
as we examine:

* Emotions, strategy and returns
* Risk, volatility and returns
* Dollar cost averaging
* Buy/sell – when and how

EXECUTING THE KIASU WAY

Remember what we have said about emotions driving bad decisions in the markets? Part of your strategy as an investor must be
to *master those emotions and use them for profit rather than loss.*

Investors in Asia (and – if we are honest – everywhere) invest based on two criteria: *Kiasu* (greed) and *kiasee* (fear). Most
investors choose the *kiasee* (fear) option simply due to the lack
of knowledge of the historic returns of the market. As we have
seen, the fear makes most investors do knee-jerk selling and

they lose money. The fear of others at a diving market will lead you to buying low to increase desirable holdings in your long-term account.

It is important not to confuse your emotions and your long-term objectives. As I stated earlier, Emotional Intelligence (EQ) is just as important in investment decisions as in business, personal relationships and life in general. There is an ancient proverb that states, "He who rules his emotions is greater than he who takes a city."

Many may say that their investment strategy is centered on the concept of attempting to lower or reduce volatility as much as possible. If risk is to be avoided, then surely volatility (which is defined as 'risk' by the MPT) should be avoided as well.

Truth be told, volatility is not risk. You know that now. We have discussed the advantages you can reap from watching for volatility. Remember that volatility is a long-term investor's friend and as such, it should not be feared, but embraced as an ally.

DOLLAR-COST-AVERAGING

One of the most efficient mechanisms in investing today is Dollar-Cost-Averaging (DCA), which *requires* volatility in order to help you out. However, DCA can be taken an important step further. Nepsis Capital Management™ in Minneapolis, Minnesota has trademarked the term, *Strategic Cost Averaging*™ (SCA). Nepsis educates their clients on the notion that volatility is their ally, as I keep repeating, and that SCA™ not only requires volatility, but thrives on it. In fact, as stated earlier in this book, the lack of volatility in the market is destabilizing to the economy, as (according to Hyman Minsky) no one would do anything else in the economy but simply invest in the financial markets.

"…Stability is destabilizing" means that relative tranquility encourages more risk-taking and innovative behavior that increases income, even as it disrupts the conditions that generate "coherency" and "tranquility." That is, the market forces that operate when a system is stable will push it towards instability, so that even if anything like an equilibrium could be achieved, it would set off behavioral responses that would quickly move the economy away from equilibrium."[xii]

So, imagine that you're given the choice between:

* Investing $1,000 in an instrument with a *fixed* 8 percent annual return each year for three years, or
* Investing $1,000 in an instrument that has *averaged* an 8 percent annual return over the same period, but has historically been volatile and earning a positive return in some years and a negative return in others.

Which would you choose? I'd imagine that most people would choose the one with a fixed return. In fact, that's likely the one I would have chosen at one time as well. The fixed rate still feels rather attractive – safe. Dealing with uncertainty is difficult, so it's nice to know exactly what you're going to get. However we need to remember this rule:

Greater Volatility = Greater Returns

If the volatile investment continues to earn an 8 percent annual return on *average* – even though its year-by-year returns fluctuate a great deal – the volatile investment is going to earn you more money. Greater volatility means a potential for greater returns.

DCA and SCA™ don't necessarily seem intuitive, so let's look at the math. [Please note that the following analysis applies only when you are doing a DCA – dollar cost averaging – of an investment.]

SCENARIO 1
The following chart shows our zero-volatility example. You will be investing $1,000 per year, and the investment will be earning exactly 8 percent each year. As you can see, at the end of the period, you will have invested $3,000, and it will have turned into $3,506.

* Average return earned by the investment: 8 percent
* Volatility: Very little to none
* Amount of money at the end: $3,506.11
* Return earned on your investment: 8 percent

	Year 1	Year 2	Year 3	Year 4
Share Price	100.00	108.00	116.64	125.97
Invested	1,000.00	1,000.00	1,000.00	
Shares Purchased	10.00	9.23	8.57	
Total Shares Owned	10.00	19.26	27.83	27.83
Total Value	1,000.00	2,080.00	3,246.40	3,506.11

Source: The Kiasu way of Investing : The correlation between volatility and returns

SCENARIO 2
This next chart shows you are still investing $1,000 per year in the stock, in a scenario in which the investment still averaged the same exact 8 percent annual return. (That is, it still started at a $100 share price and three years later had a share price of $125.97.)

However, in this scenario, in years two and three, the investment fluctuated in price from our base-line 8 percent scenario. This time, instead of the share price in year two being $108, it was $128 (or $20 higher). And in year three, instead of $116.64, it was $96.64 ($20 lower). Again, this directly affects the number of new shares you purchase each year.

- Average return earned by the investment: 8 percent
- Volatility: $20 upward, followed by $20 downward (over the previous scenario)
- Amount of money at the end: $3,547.34
- Return earned on your investment: 8.62 percent

	Year 1	Year 2	Year 3	Year 4
Share Price	100.00	128.00	96.64	125.97
Invested	1,000.00	1,000.00	1,000.00	
Shares Purchased	10.00	7.81	10.35	
Total Shares Owned	10.00	17.81	28.16	28.16
Total Value	1,000.00	2,280.00	2,721.40	3,547.34

Source: The Kiasu way of Investing : The correlation between volatility and returns

As you can see, adding some volatility into the scenario did in fact increase your return. In short, this is because dollar cost averaging into a volatile investment sets you up to automatically take advantage of price swings by buying more shares when the price is low.

Okay, so volatility helps your return in that scenario. But what about in other situations? For example, what happens when the price swings happen in the other order (downward first, followed by upward)?

SCENARIO 3

This third scenario is the same as Scenario 2, but with downward volatility first, followed by upward volatility. So with the share price in year two at $88, you can purchase more than double the number of shares you started with. In year three, you buy fewer shares – but your goal here is to play with the volatility, so you go ahead and purchase 7 or so shares. The share price ends at $125.97 in year four, as in the previous scenarios.

- Average return earned by the investment: 8 percent
- Volatility: Great volatility with $20 downward, followed by $20 upward
- Amount of money at the end: $3,613.09
- Return earned on your investment: 9.59 percent

	Year 1	Year 2	Year 3	Year 4
Share Price	100.00	88.00	136.64	125.97
Invested	1,000.00	1,000.00	1,000.00	
Shares Purchased	10.00	11.36	7.32	
Total Shares Owned	10.00	21.36	28.68	28.68
Total Value	1,000.00	1,880.00	3,919.13	3,613.09

Source: The Kiasu way of Investing : The correlation between volatility and returns

As you can see, the results are even better here than in Scenario 2. So far, we can conclude that some volatility is better than no volatility and that it is beneficial regardless of the order in which it occurs.

What happens when we increase the volatility further?

SCENARIO 4
Scenario 4 is the same as Scenario 2, except that the volatility is greater.

Average return earned by the investment: 8 percent

- Volatility: $50 upward, followed by $50 downward
- Amount of money at the end: $3,947.28
- Return earned on your investment: 14.36 percent

	Year 1	Year 2	Year 3	Year 4
Share Price	100.00	158.00	66.64	125.97
Invested	1,000.00	1,000.00	1,000.00	
Shares Purchased	10.00	6.33	15.01	
Total Shares Owned	10.00	16.33	31.34	31.34
Total Value	1,000.00	2,580.00	2,088.17	3,947.28

Source: The Kiasu way of Investing : The correlation between volatility and returns

Wow, look at that return! Earning a 14 percent return on your money while investing in something that only gained 8 percent over the period (when we look purely at share price of year one and share price at year four) is pretty impressive.

The conclusion? Simply that using volatility through a disciplined process such as DCA or SCA™ can potentially enhance returns over time, even when your first year's returns are negative. This is due to the fact you are strategically buying more shares when the share price is low and fewer or no shares when the price is high.[xiii]

Of course, there are no guarantees of success utilizing this method. However, when the investment process includes investing in quality companies, DCA or SCA™ can be a tremendous benefit to long-term investing.

At the end of the day, increased volatility simply creates a situation in which the market lows are lower, thereby making the investment process more effective. Hence, greater volatility can equate to greater returns. You must fully understand that the volatility of the stock market isn't just something you have to put up with in order to earn superior returns; it's actually an essential factor that directly improves your returns.

Volatility creates opportunities. Opportunities create wealth.

Look at market fluctuations – volatility – as your friend rather than your enemy; profit from other market participants' folly rather than participating in it!

WHY DOES VOLATILITY INCREASE RETURNS?

A note here on bear markets (a market term for recessions/depressions, when market prices drop): *The market has always bounced back.* Even following the Great Depression, it bounced back (obviously, since here we are with a higher market).

In the book '"*Stocks for the Long Run*" by Professor Jeremy Siegel[xiv], he wrote, "Over the 210 years one examines stock market returns, the real return on a broadly diversified portfolio of stock has averaged 6.6 percent per year. This means that, on average, a diversified stock portfolio … has nearly doubled in purchasing power every decade over the past two centuries." During the same period, "the average real return on *gold* has been only 0.7% per year. In the long run, gold prices have remained just ahead of the inflation rate, but little more."

When you're doing dollar cost averaging into an investment, you're automatically buying more shares when the market is low, and fewer/none when the market is high – and as shown in our scenarios above, you reap the benefits of high-low fluctuations. You don't pay attention to the stock market as a whole – not at all. Why not? You are not buying *stocks*!

Remember: You are buying companies. Companies chosen for their strength and performance *over the long run*.

When you enhance with the strategy of SCA™ (not shown in my scenarios), you can potentially improve on those returns over time by also investing more during unforeseen market or company events (that is, not just once a year as I have shown).

Increased volatility simply creates multiple situations in which the market lows are lower, and market highs are higher, thereby making your DCA (or even better, your SCA™) more effective over a period of time.

ARE YOU A TRADER?

I believe a word about the difference between a *trader* and an *investor* is in order at this point in our conversation.

Michael Lewis' book, *"Flash Boys: A Wall Street Revolt"* gives us an excellent picture of a *trader*. A trader is looking for a fast (even "flash" speed) in-and-out profit. An institutional trader loads up on high-priced technology (in the millions of dollars' worth) that allows him to perform nanosecond or "flash" buy/sell transactions from his trading screen. This trader is looking for someone like you to pay his in-out fees; providing you with an actual profit is not on his horizon; he only looks for his own profit. Such a trader has no interest in the instrument he has flashed in-and-out of, and certainly does not consider himself an owner of that company. You can call him a Wall Street Boy or a high-speed trader, but either way he has "traded ahead" (of you and the markets). The high-speed trader is involved in things like 'latency arbitrage' where the trader takes advantage of price disparities between the same or related securities on different markets. The effect is the same – he's in it for frequent, small (or not-so-small) profits, made in a heartbeat, so that he can move on to the next flash-profit opportunity.

An *investor* is what you and I have been talking about in this book. An investor is in it for long-term profits that outperform the markets; he is in it for company ownership. An investor is in it for all the company's stellar and long-term fundamentals. An investor is willing to understand the core product or service, to understand how the company looks in the marketplace over the coming decade(s), to look at the management team and its effectiveness. The investor rests easy at night. He is not worried about the fees he's paid to buy more of his favorite companies because he knows his buy strategy will cover them and even more. He is not worried about a minor or temporary shift in the greater market or even watching for them like the flash trader, because he is not playing those minute-by-minute shifts – but only the long-term.

WHEN TO SELL

By now, you are surely asking yourself about selling any single item in your portfolio. I know you are curious about this, because you know that you have only "made real money" once you sell your company – once you liquidate a profitable holding.

Yes, your portfolio manager needs a *Sell Philosophy* and some rules to go by – just as he has a *Buy Philosophy* ensuring you of long-term profits.

I've spoken about the Buying Philosophy, and will do so some more in these pages. But rest assured, we understand that there is a need to monitor your portfolio to make the occasional ad-justment. The adjustments will not always be to purchase more of your companies through dollar cost averaging! Sometimes, you need to sell.

However, we never sell just because the greater market takes a temporary downturn or upturn. We never sell because of fear or from greed, either. There are really only 4 **_Rules of Action_** to sell off companies you have been holding in your portfolio. Here they are in a nutshell:

1. The *long-term fundamentals* of the company you are hold-ing, or of its sector as a whole, have changed. Perhaps they have disintegrated.
2. A *potentially better opportunity* has come into our awareness and we need to make room for it. That is, you need the cash to purchase those other shares.

3. We sell a *portion* of a position to *lock in gains* and/or *re-balance your portfolio.* One of your companies has done so well that it represents a too-large percentage of your portfolio for the original balance you created. So you sell off some of it to buy more of your other great companies.
4. *Tax management* issues. These are highly individual and we hope, as financial and investment advisors, that you inform us of all the components of your wealth and assets so that we may help do things tax-efficiently for you.

Please understand: There's really only one proven profitable strategy available to the individual or retail *investor.* That is the **buy-and-hold strategy**. You can try day-trading with some of your cash, sure, to have some fun; you can even trade on weekly or monthly plays on an Internet platform. But at the end of the day, it will seem the markets are against you. In fact, if they seem to largely favor the institutional traders, who are as we have said loaded with high-tech tools allowing them to place nanosecond trades in-and-out, that leaves only one strategy for any serious individual investor:

> **Buy** *after solid analysis of the fundamentals;* **hold** *for the very long term; periodically* **review** *with a dispassionate mindset and sell only from the above* **4 rules of action***.*

<u>*Rule of Action #1*</u> acknowledges that, yes, things do change in our marketplace. Industries and/or the companies within them evolve in reaction to any number of stimuli. Looking at the company and industry fundamentals from time to time is essential to keeping up with the ramifications of those stimuli. Technology may cause one industry to fail or evolve out of the marketplace or its original product lines entirely; history shows us any number of examples. Foreign competition for a formerly-strong US industry may have a similar effect. We watch; we gauge whether the change is in the long-term fundamentals or is only a passing fancy.

Rules of Action #2 and #3 acknowledge this: No single company in our portfolio makes up the majority of the portfolio performance. It is the portfolio *allocation* that is most important on a long-term basis. As we employ DCA and SCA strategies of repurchase of companies, we may find we have created a lopsided holding. We can correct as opportunities to lock in gains arise. We can rebalance by adding a new company that looks like a new long-term opportunity, as we examine its fundamentals in view to a long-term buy-and-hold.

Rule of Action #4 is quite personal to your individual investment goals, your total wealth, and the types of assets you currently hold in all your accounts. Your advisor will be checking in with you about those issues and your tax management objectives.

In all cases, "knowing what you own" is still a rule of thumb. It protects you from chasing the latest new thing from greed and from selling from fear. Treating your portfolio as though you are full owner of each business gives you a long-range perspective that emotional investors or traders do not have.

The portfolio manager's outlook on selling ultimately comes down to whether or not the sale will continue to push the portfolio of the investor in the right direction.

LESSONS LEARNED
If you're following a portfolio management strategy of *Dollar Cost Average* or *Strategic Cost Average*™ for your investments, greater volatility can mean greater returns for you. In other words,

the volatility of the stock market isn't just something you have to 'put up with' in order to earn superior returns. It's actually an essential tool for you to actively use, that directly improves your return. Likewise, having guidelines – a strategy – for when and how to sell any of your holdings can increase your overall returns, and certainly avoid great losses.

So we've looked at the first 2 Keys: philosophy and strategy. We've looked at when to do any selling, to reassure you that corrective and profit-taking measures are really a part of our philosophy and strategy.

And this leads us to the next Key for Successful Investing – having a manager whose hands are not tied up in trading-house rules and products. Having a portfolio manager who is free to act in your interests. Let's see how it is helpful for your invest- ment advisor to have *flexibility*.

Unfettered Flexibility for Your Money Manager

❧

THIS THIRD STEP TO ACHIEVING highest potential returns from your investment portfolio calls for providing the *flexibility* your manager needs to do tax efficient management, as well as to turn market volatility into an ally that gives your portfolio holdings higher returns over the long run. This flexibility includes:

- Freedom from funds and from in-house product constraints and style box investment
- Freedom to pursue investment opportunity wherever it should arise
- Tax efficient management of your portfolio holdings and returns

Are you with the right money manager? What is it that would make you change managers? Perhaps some of the information in this section will help you rethink not only who manages your money – but how. It might show you that you need to be more hands-on than you thought.

HAND CUFFS

Why is your money manager constrained to a certain bench-mark, peer group or prospectus objective? Research done by the University of Denver and *ICON Advisors* emphatically states that the "style box" type of investing constrains a manager's ability to manage money and – by thus limiting their flexibility – causes severe underperformance.[xv]

What is a 'style box'? It is *fixed* types of investment that a style box manager must make for you if you are his client. Current practice has most money managers obliged by their firm or bank to present only a particular style box or category of investments option. One such style box could be only Small Cap Value stocks; another style box could be only International stocks. Investment banks likewise have their "house products" which are really just style boxes in disguise and which also almost always reduce your returns. The system imposed by boxes seems rational, but it lacks flexibility. There is no opportunity within the box for the advisor to take advantage of opportunities *outside* the box for you, which is contrary to the ultimate objective of investing.

As research shows, this style box system has absolutely no proven basis, but has simply evolved out of convenience – to the money management firms. These academic studies have concluded that "boxing in" a portfolio and a portfolio manager can increase volatility to your detriment and reduce your returns (that is, if you see increased volatility and do not have a *strategy* to take profitable advantage of it as I have described elsewhere). In fact, *Morningstar,* which introduced its nine-box grid in 1992, has said that the boxes were never intended to *construct a portfolio.*

University of Denver Tom Howard, co-founder, CEO and head of research at *Athena Invest,* examined the issue of style boxes. Dr. Howard's study revealed that active managers sacrifice, on average, 300 basis points (3 percent) of performance in their efforts to remain true to their style/size category, a figure they say is backed up by similar studies from other sources.

Several of these studies also indicate that diversifying amongst style boxes *does not necessarily ensure risk reduction*, which is the often-cited benefit.

Styles boxes were designed to evaluate and monitor investments, not to be a rigid framework for asset allocation. Remember that when you sense that your money manager is proposing one to you!

You don't want your money manager wearing the hand cuffs his firm (or his own thinking) locked on him! You don't want to wear them, either!

The investment process should be driven by its philosophy and strategy. It must not be driven by whether it fits in a style box or not. If your portfolio management is driven by your agreed, specific investment philosophy and strategy, adding this flexibility allows the investor to

- avoid "cookie-cutter" investing
- avoid the limitations set on portfolios
- utilize the power of SCA™ (and DCA, dollar cost averaging) to not only potentially enhance portfolio performance, but also
- allow for greater flexibility in tax-efficiency in an investor's portfolio.

STYLE BOX

Equity Style Box | **Fixed Income Style Box**

	Value	Blend	Growth		Short	Interm	Long	
Large					■			**High**
Medium								**Medium**
Small			■					**Low**

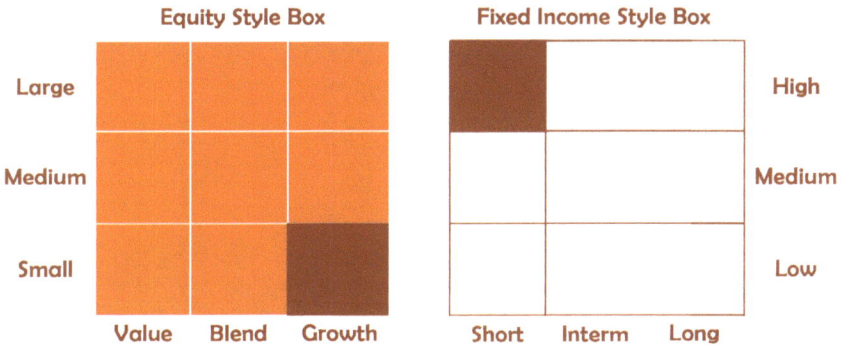

Source: Investopedia

PENNY JAR

Your portfolio manager makes use of the process they call a "penny jar theory" when they use the 4 Keys to Successful Investing. The penny jar approach is a way for them to invest in companies over time, freely, according to which opportunities present profits over the long-term and regardless of any style-boxing. You start out purchasing the few shares you can afford in a great company, and you go on to accumulate more shares in that company over time (remember volatility, which can allow you to buy low). In other words, you put in a few pennies at first, and a few more periodically as your purchase criteria are met – your penny jar gets fuller as you come into owning more and more shares of your favored companies.

If you go with the portfolio manager who is free to invest for you as a result of having Total Clarity™ and by following the four keys of successful investing, you will have a manager acting from honesty and confidence on your behalf. You stay with a portfolio manager who has an investment strategy that you can understand with clarity. You partner with a manager who has a true commitment to transparency – allowing you, the investor, to fully understand what you own and why, bringing you to Total Clarity™ in all your investment choices.

LESSONS LEARNED

Flexibility is required both to pursue compelling opportunities and to minimize risk. Money managers require:

- a sound philosophy and strategy which you understand and agree with,
- the ability to invest in great long-term opportunities for you with unfettered flexibility, and
- a vision that extends beyond artificial boxes.

Furthermore, stock selection should be based on a company's ability *to deliver long-term value to shareholders*, not on staying in a style box.

Managers that focus on a philosophy and strategy-based investing rather than an arbitrary "style box" requirements have greater flexibility and provide higher returns to you with lower risk over the long-term.

SCA™ can provide the flexibility allowing the stock market's volatility to be an investor's friend. And flexibility allows for tax efficient management of a portfolio.

Hiring a Money Manager Who Provides Transparency

❧

A LEVEL OF *TRANSPARENCY* IN your portfolio will guide your investment decisions by helping you understand what you own and why you own it. Transparency allows you to:

⁍ Have the facts about what you own
⁍ Know why you own it
⁍ Identify emotional codependency and eliminate it
⁍ Know if it is 'news' (fact) or just noise (entertainment)
⁍ Embrace uncertainty, by not acting on your greed and fear feelings when these get momentarily stirred up
⁍ Avoid fanciful comparing or predicting – inform yourself instead with facts

Do you know exactly where each of your tax dollars goes – what it is used to pay for or provide? Of course not! There is no factual information about this readily available to us. There is no *transparency* or clarity. Transparency is having knowledge and getting facts. It is Total Clarity™. You need transparency as you look at your portfolio. You need this transparency from your advisors.

Do you know which companies you own in your portfolio? As an investor in a company's stock, you are an <u>owner of that</u>

<u>business</u>. I like to underscore that to my clients – it is your key to gaining the best perspective you can on your investment choices. A vast majority of investors have no idea of their number one portfolio holding, much less the names of other stocks they own. If you don't know the names of your investments, you cannot know much about that company, either. You don't know its fundamentals and thus, have no certainty it will yield you any profits. This has been one of the themes of this book: **Know what you own.**

I believe there is nothing worse than not knowing what you own and why you own it. For instance, when a company's stock price unexpectedly goes down, was it due to *outside* market forces or because of fundamental changes *within* the company? Is the situation one of a damaged stock or damaged company? Stocks are damaged by the stock market. Companies are damaged by the firm's management.

When investors are naive as to what they own and why they own it, they are not in a position to make rational decisions. If you are not familiar with the companies behind the stocks, you cannot fully understand your portfolio.

The great British economist John Maynard Keynes stated, "As time goes on, I get more and more convinced that the right method in investment is to put fairly large sums into enterprises which one thinks one knows something about and in the management of which one thoroughly believes." Decades ago, this guru was stating the same thing!

I believe that today's investors are bedeviled by myopic (short) time horizons. Almost everywhere you look in society, we seem to have an encounter with the short-term. We want results now. We want to measure our portfolio's returns on a weekly basis, then monthly and so on. Advisors, consultants and money managers, too, want to measure performance on increasingly short-time horizons.

What causes this phenomenon? I contend that it comes directly from the premise that investors simply do not know what they own and why they own it.

Opaque Funds

Mutual funds are emphatically *not* designed to be transparent. Your current advisor started by selling you Class A mutual fund shares with its front-end <u>sales charge</u> of 4.75 percent to 6.00 percent in the late 1990s. (Class A shares often still have a 0.25 percent per year asset-based sales charge.) Then, in the early years of the 2000s, your advisor went on to sell you a Class C mutual fund with its recurring 1 percent annual asset-based sales charges that you typically <u>do not see</u> unless you sell your mutual funds within the first year of ownership. This was because investment advisors had to compete with no-load mutual funds, and the public objected to paying advisors high upfront sales charges.

The *Investment Act of 1940* structured mutual funds in a way that leaves the investor uncertain as to when and why a money manager bought or sold a position. Uncertainty is the opposite of transparency. This lack of transparency has led to extremely dramatic changes in the way people approach investing. Remember what we said about Emotional IQ: Research irrefutably states that people by nature will succumb to emotions such as fear and greed when presented with an unknown in intense situations. When they do not know what they own and why they own it, their emotions take over, discipline goes out the window. And what is left? Highly irrational actions are taken – typically an excessive amount of trading. That trading was only about buying high and selling low!

Research done by Dr. KW Macro and *Bogle Research* in 2005 shows that as the investment world has moved to being consumed by "packaged products" (and thus a lack of transparency, such as in mutual funds), holding stock over a long-term has gone down dramatically. As the chart below shows, before the giant move to mutual funds in 1960, the average holding period of New York Stock Exchange (NYSE) listed stocks was 8 years. Today, it stands at 11 months, as you see in the graph. [xvi] We seek immediate results in vain. We don't have the knowledge, information and Total Clarity™ it takes to be patient for that result! We don't know our companies as we bounce from one Buy High-Sell Low investment to the next. Where is the transparency?

What has happened is that the investor has abandoned the attitude of being an owner in a business. He has moved into being a speculator, reacting from his fear and greed as drivers of his investment decision-making. This harkens back to investors not knowing why they own or what they own.

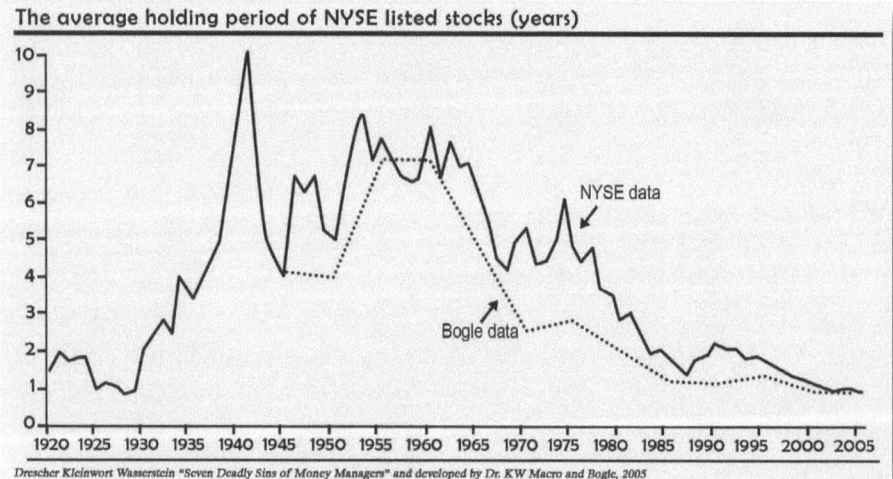

The average holding period of NYSE listed stocks (years)

Drescher Kleinwort Wasserstein "Seven Deadly Sins of Money Managers" and developed by Dr. KW Macro and Bogle, 2005

WHAT IS A CODEPENDENT RELATIONSHIP?

Good investor behavior is something that must be developed. So few people start out as 'natural' investors for the long-term. Emotions play a huge role here. Emotional IQ is important for all investors to self-manage, especially as regards the fear-greed feelings that inevitably get stirred up as we hear about market movements. We can look first to codependent relationships between investor and advisor as a way that investors try to mitigate emotions.

The first step is to understand the meaning of this codependent relationship, then put it in the context of your investments and your dealings with financial advisors.

Experts say codependency is a pattern of behavior in which you find yourself dependent on approval from someone else for your self-worth, self-confidence and identity. Amongst the key characteristics of codependency, the most common is an excessive reliance on other people for approval (as in "Yes, this decision you made is great!") and identity (as in "Yes, you are a hard worker and a very smart investor!").

I would say there is a definite codependent relationship between institutional investment firms and the retail (individual) investor.

Codependency came to light for me about 10 years ago when I decided to leave the big wire house brokerage firm where I was working. I was confused by the decision of a few clients not to follow me into independence, although I had many clients that been with me since the 1990s. When I got into this business, I discovered that some clients are more concerned about staying with a big name brokerage firm because it helps boost their ego, or helps them fulfill a sense of self-worth that they have somehow made it to the big time. I presumed they'd rather have a portfolio manager who follows a specific philosophy and strategy for not only managing money, but in earning good returns! Some investors simply need a big wire house brokerage house to feel good about themselves. This is codependency, *regardless of investment results.*

The retail investor who feels they are unable to take care of themselves will assign loyalty to a certain money manager or giant retail investment firm if they feel they can get their emotional needs met. This is big with professionals – they are, after all, on the other side of the codependency! The money manager or financial advisor – who needs to feel a sense of self-worth himself – is more than happy to oblige.

So the investor needs certainty, attention and approval, and the manager needs to show off his expertise and experience. Another aspect of a codependent relationship has been called "prediction addiction". This means that the advisor welcomes questions like from his prediction-hungry clients:

* Where do you think the market is going?
* What is going to happen to the price of oil?
* What is the Fed going to do with interest rates?

The financial advisor feeds her own desire for self-worth not only by boldly answering all the questions (even though no one can predict the future), but by providing even more informational "noise" about what the investor asks. Thus, this dysfunctional relationship has begun.

Getting more information from your advisor does not equate to greater knowledge for you. The following points highlight this:

* We tend to equate information and knowledge as one and the same, even though they are actually two different things. Remember 'noise versus news'.

- Numerous studies show that increasing information (e.g.: economic data) leads to increased confusion rather than increased accuracy! Too much information can be detrimental to the decision-making process.

Daniel G Bornstein, 20th century American author and historian, in his book "*The Discoverers*" said, "The greatest obstacle to discovery is not ignorance – but the illusion of knowledge."

This codependent relationship between individual investor and financial advisor is just that – comforting each other with the illusion of knowledge… instead of focusing on a few sound principles of learning factually about the businesses we hold for the long run.

I always think it's a humorous codependency trait that investors from a small town will drive two or three counties over to work with a financial advisor from a big city. This translates in the Caribbean this way: investors of the Caribbean feel special that a financial advisor from Puerto Rico or the states flies in to see them. Both scenarios lead the investor to believe a certain advisor has some special knowledge or a Midas Touch.

The only question that the investor should be concerned about is, "What is the financial advisor's philosophy, strategy and transparency for the investing he does for me?"

This desire for certainty through predictions manifests itself variously:

- Most people are in denial regarding uncertainty – they believe that one system or another out there (software; strategies; etc.) is capable of moving them into 100 percent certainty
- Most people believe they can win in Las Vegas or even the lottery – even though the odds are largely stacked against it

- Most people believe they are luckier than the other guy – but that is mostly ego
- Most people falsely presume that the unpredictable can be reliably forecast – they'd like to believe that everything can eventually be known

Soothsayers (Obeah men), economic forecasters and weatherman – and financial talking heads on televisions – keep their jobs because the general public is addicted to prediction. Just another type of codependency.

When we assign certainty to events like predicting the future or of being luckier than others, we allow ourselves (especially in this case of Wall Street), to be lulled into a false sense of security. This perpetual state of codependency permits the investor to feed off the overconfident financial advisor whose predictions are almost always presented with authority. Sadly, it causes the investor to make the wrong decision, almost always at the wrong time. It is always *his* loss, not the advisor's!

What would happen if the financial advisor actually embraced uncertainty as opposed to denying its very existence? What would happen if they actually admitted they could not predict the future?

Embracing uncertainty, although counterintuitive, actually reduces risk in the decision-making process.

- I am honest with myself and my investors when I say I cannot predict the future. The foundation of the relationship is no longer codependency, as I seek the best interest of both my investors and my firm.
- I am now free to base my decision-making process on factual information and not speculation.
- Right perspectives, such as ownership through stock of a business, are the best path to generating wealth over

the long-term. In any given year, 70 percent of publicly traded businesses will have a positive return.

❧ My investment portfolio of well-run businesses is only one amongst multiple sources of income in the overall wealth-building strategy.

❧ My process is based upon probabilistic science versus speculative prediction. Hence, I reduce the risks as I prepare my portfolio for the unknown, as opposed to falsely believing I have it covered (due to a false certainty of the outcome).

❧ I obtain wisdom and understanding if I admit that I simply do not know what I do not know. This healthy respect for uncertainty drives us to improvement and causes us to refine our judgments, as we acknowledge we do not know it all.

❧ Lastly, embracing uncertainty limits us to question conventional thinking and the status quo – as you begin to see with clarity what others do not.

The next component of the emotional and codependent relationship between Wall Street and Main Street is driven by both sides' insatiable appetite to 'keep up with the Joneses.'[xvii]

Comparison with others is the cause of more unhappiness in the world than anything else, and stirs up lust and greed – and fear we will fall behind our peers. Comparison-created unhappiness and insecurity seems driven by a basic principle that whatever we have is enough – until we see someone else who has more!

Another feeling associated with this keeping-up phenomenon is impatience. Investors exhibit it and advisors thrive on it. Here is how this aspect of codependency works: Comparison with others' results is the main reason why investors have trouble patiently sitting on their hands, letting whatever process they are comfortable with work for them. If you tell a client that they made 12 percent on their account, they are pleased – until they learn that "everyone else" made 14 percent!

The whole financial services industry, as it is constructed, is predicated on making investors upset (impatient, greedy, fearful) so that you move your money around in a frenzy. They really want you to panic, become fearful and move that cash elsewhere. Why? Money in motion creates fees and commissions for the financial firms, of course! 90 percent of the clients that come to us come from other financial advisors. The creation of more and more benchmarks and style boxes is nothing more than the creation of more things to compare to, allowing clients to stay in a perpetual state of outrage, panic and motion.

Comparison-created unhappiness as mentioned earlier caused by the desire to 'keep up with the Joneses' in the investment world is pervasive. All we have to do is just look at benchmarking peer group rankings, star ratings and the like – they are nothing more than comparisons.

So, if in the codependent scenario that you have established, your financial advisor said to you that last year you earned 10 percent on your portfolio – do you think you would be pleased? These codependent behaviors most people have would lead them to answer by saying, "That depends." That depends on what you find out about others' returns. You see that the market earned 14 percent, but the average money manager earned 13 percent, and your portfolio only earned 10 percent? Then you feel a sense of betrayal and ultimately dissatisfaction or unhappiness. The result may be that you seek out a higher-performing advisor.

Emotion-based comparisons are one of the main reasons why both advisors and investors have trouble allowing whatever process they originally selected to work for them.

COSTLY EMOTIONS

Back in 2012, W. Michael Robertson, chairman of *Robertson Wealth Management* of Houston, predicted in one of his talks that stocks would start to fall in June of that year. He remarked, as many have, that personal spending in the U.S. is typically about 70 percent of the economy. He expressed the strong belief that baby boomers' personal spending specifically would drop quite a lot, as they got older and had fewer wants and needs to spend on. Robertson saw that as a huge risk to the stability of the American economy, since baby boomers are such a huge population in numbers of spenders.

The effect of that dire prediction was fear and anxiety in the listeners, because they bought the story hook, line and sinker. After all, the fellow was an expert. After the talk, people announced outright that they would sell their holdings – cash in and hunker down for the economic catastrophe. If I know human nature, more than one did this without saying so out loud.

Persuasive as it sometimes sounds, investing based on the feelings that these types of predictions stir up in you can cost you dearly in portfolio returns! Listening to predictions – whose only goal, if we are honest, is to stir up either greed or fear in us – and then acting on the fear or greed that results within us is a pricey, expensive error.

It is so tempting to listen and react emotionally to all of these so-called experts who predict this or that boom or bust. What is worse is when we follow a television talking head's predictions and go into greed or fear, too! Remember that almost no television financial reporter is a finance or investing expert – they are journalists.

WHY WE LISTEN TO FORECASTS

In his book, '*Your Money and Your Brain: How the New Science of Neuro-Economics Can Help Make You Rich*', financial writer Jason

Zweig says that there's a natural sort of compulsion on the part of humans to make forecasts. He calls such compulsions the "prediction addiction." It would seem that humans are obsessive about finding and making sense of patterns, he says. This would be where we get our propensity not only to make but to ask for forecasts in any arena we are active in.

Unfortunately, we usually think we have discovered predictability where none actually exists. This is what those economic and investing clairvoyants, forecasters and sooth-sayers are doing when they come up with their statements.

Investors with financial advisors think they are paying us to make such predictions. My fellow advisors and I must face facts – we cannot. And the best ones don't. Look at it this way: If you cannot make a prediction, neither can we. All financial advisors can do is teach you to think like a business owner and be the owner of businesses with a long-term approach to investing.

For my clients and me it's *never* a right time to sell, as we want to hold on to certain companies forever if we can. My clients do not ask me what I think stocks will do for the rest of the year, they already know what my answer is – I will always say, "I don't know and we're in this for the long haul."

Prophecies and predictions are costly. Beware. Sit tight and wait them out.

NOT KNOWING

To show the destructiveness of acting on predictions, I will go back to what I have already said about mutual funds and about admitting "I don't know". If a potential client walks into my office and shows me their portfolio of mutual funds, I explain my own analysis of mutual funds and why they should not own them:

- There is no transparency.
- There are (by the law of great numbers) a number of non-performing or negatively performing stocks in the fund. I don't want those, but cannot toss them out.
- I can't understand the fundamentals of each and every stock. There are too many eggs in this basket.

The only case I could ever make for owning any is if they are on the fixed income side of the portfolio and the mutual funds are being used for added *efficiency* in the portfolio. I end up showing that investors really fare worse than the fund's announced return rate. No predictions; just facts based on science, common sense and historic data. Human nature seeks out what has performed well in the past and reaches the seemingly logical conclusion that the same actions will lead again to a great performance.

Carl Richards, author of '*The Behavior Gap: Simple Ways to Stop Doing Dumb Things with Money*', writes that people will "repeat [a dumb or ineffective behavior] until broke." He says, "When people ask me to predict the future, I always just chuckle and say 'I have no idea.'" Most people, he says, know that we don't know and find it refreshing when we admit it.

I tell my clients that, while I can't predict the markets, I can *know* something almost as valuable – human behavior. I can tell them with near-perfect certainty that, if stocks go up over the next year, people will move into stocks. And if stocks do poorly, people will pull money out of them. I tell clients that *rebalancing* is the one way to be a true contrarian, and since everyone loves to be a contrarian, I explain how that rebalancing will work.

Accepting that the future is uncertain can be a very lonely feeling. Getting our clients to accept that uncertainty, with the understanding that we don't know how markets will perform, isn't easy. In investing, knowing that we *don't* know is one of the keys to avoiding herd behavior – and increasing returns.[xviii]

Breaking Free of Money-Losing Behaviors

Emotional self-comparison in the investment world – from fear, greed and other strong emotions – leads to very unsound decision-making, both on the investment side (your side) and money management side (your advisor) of the equation.

The really big question is how you can break free from the addictive forces of this relationship that you might be stuck in. I realize that this is not easy, as the force of our emotional needs can be hard to shake off. I recommend doing the following:

- Stop equating more news with more knowledge and wisdom. Eradicate the "noise of news" and separate the wheat from the chaff. Get knowledge – facts – from solid, proven sources. In fact, just turn off the news programs, because now you know that … they don't know!
- Be observant and watchful for useful volatility, without allowing fear and greed caused by investor gossip and news media to affect your decision-making process.
- Stop chasing after those that pretend to predict the future.
- Understand your Emotional IQ in the situation. Ask, "Am I doing this from panic or from knowledge?"
- Lastly, stop comparing your investment performance to that of market benchmarks, other money managers, or even to results of coworkers, family and friends. Set your own goals with your own financial advisor and allow him to do the job.

I believe that the cycle of codependency that has existed can be broken for investors who are fed up with unfulfilled promises. The power is in your hands, so go and do the right thing. Shake off the news media and the emotion-stirring messages that they send through all media channels. Look for and expect transparency from your advisor.

Remember that speaking with any certainty actually increases risk in the decision-making process. On the other hand, admitting to uncertainty actually decreases risk. When financial advisors are asked what the market is doing going to do, we should simply respond with an "I don't know", because we really don't know answer to that question.[xix] Asked if you will have available free cash to add to a holding at the next downturn, answer with an "I don't know yet." And you'll be right.

LESSONS LEARNED

This section has been about knowing yourself in addition to knowing what you own. Knowing your emotional reactions to things is vital to controlling those emotions that would have you make disastrous financial decisions. When you let go of the momentary fears or greed, you can more easily stick with your long-term investment plan – you do it dispassionately, not emotionally.

Human behavior and emotions are much, much more predictable than what may happen in the markets, so what you need to do is remember that greed and fear are not feelings you should make investment decisions from!

Knowing what you own and having a sound strategy for investing allows you to sleep at night. You have chosen to be owner of great companies. Great companies do not disappear with one dire prediction – in fact, they usually laugh them off and prove them wrong. Take comfort in that. Have a great enough number of companies in your portfolio for diversification, but few enough that you know about the companies. Prefer knowledge about them to predictions. Embrace uncertainty, because you know that this is what brings you the opportunities for growing your profits!

Don't listen to television financial news and those talking heads – it is just of entertainment value, and not much of that! It is noise that can all too often stir up greed or fear and tempt you to leave your clear strategies behind.

Remember what *you* know about those soothsayers: They <u>don't</u> know. Even when they say they do!

Conclusion

No one said it better than John Maynard Keynes when he commented, "The spectacle of modern investment markets has sometimes moved me towards the conclusion that to make the purchase of an investment permanent and indissoluble like marriage, except by reason of death … or other grave cause, might be a useful remedy for our contemporary evils. For this would force the investor to direct his mind to the long-term prospects and to those only." Keynes said this in 1936. Wow! What do you think he would have to say today?[xx]

At the end of each day, as the closing bell rings, every money manager, Registered Investment Advisor and individual investor should reflect on their decisions. Was there a regular pattern, reason, or logic to the decisions made today? If not, you should really reconsider your strategy, or lack thereof. This is why I have proposed to you this Total Clarity™ approach that I know leads to successful investing.

The keys to clarity in investing are simple enough to understand, but all too easy to neglect. Take the time to re-evaluate your investment decisions and ensure that you are in Total Clarity™.

Be certain that you understand our **Four Keys to Successful Investing**. Here they are again for you:

1. A back-to-basics **philosophy** centered on clarity that has the validation of long-term, historic market success.
2. An investment **strategy** that utilizes market volatility, dollar cost averaging and SCA™ in long-term investments in quality companies found in a select few sectors.
3. Providing the **flexibility** to your advisor that is needed to create a tax efficient management of a portfolio, to turn market volatility into an ally that gives you higher returns over the long run, to benefit from out-of-the-box opportunities that arise and meet your goal and strategy requirements.
4. A level of **transparency** and facts that will guide your investment decisions by helping you understand what you own and why you own it.

Also let me remind you of our **3 Favorite Corollaries**:

a) Make sure <u>you know what you own</u> and why you own it, by viewing yourself as a business *owner* not as a market speculator.
b) <u>Know why you are selling</u> and when it is best to do so. Having good sell or rebalancing strategies – and emotional control – protects your portfolio and your earned profits.
c) <u>Diversify wisely</u>. Strive not to be overly diversified and remember what Buffet warned, "Wide diversification is only required when investors do not understand what they are doing."

Contrary to the Modern Portfolio Theory (MPT), I would argue that volatility (i.e., upwards and downwards moves of the market or of your holdings) is not your enemy but your friend. Simply put, once you have chosen some great long-term companies to invest in, the volatility of the stock market is actually an *essential factor directly improving your returns.* The bottom line is work your strategy and make sure your strategy works for you!

Understand your own investment philosophy and the strategies of your chosen portfolio manager – then periodically make sure you are on the same page over the time of your investing relationship. Hiring a money manager who is unabashedly transparent with you and puts clear, transparent investment choices into your portfolio is paramount in the investing process. The bottom line is to demand that the money manager you hire is vigilant about being transparent at all times! Don't you or your advisor get caught in the style box trap. Make sure that your money managers have complete flexibility and are equipped with every tool possible to execute the strategy for which you hired them. Peer group comparisons, short-view investing, and style box or fund "handcuffing" are used as crutches for a weak investment philosophy. The current system imposed by said constraints *seem* rational and intuitive, but at the end of the day lacks flexibility, which is contrary to the ultimate objective of investing. Flexibility is required both to pursue compelling opportunities and to minimize risk. The bottom-line conclusion is to seek out a money manager who welcomes the ability to invest with unfettered flexibility and vision that extends beyond artificial peer group comparisons, style boxes and benchmarking!

There are a few money managers and investment advisors that believe that proper investment **Philosophy, Strategy, Flexibility** and **Transparency**™ can help you be a successful investor – and that is what we call Total Clarity™!

Glossary of Terms

❧

THIS IS A REVIEW OF terms used in this book, to help you better understand our topic.

1. **401(k) Plan** – Unique to the USA, this is a savings plan set up by companies for its owners and employed individuals. The number "401(k)" refers to the section of the US Tax Code which defines and manages taxation of such plans. An employer sets up a plan according to the rules of the Tax Code, allowing eligible employees may make "contributions" via salary reductions on a post-tax or pretax basis. Employers offering a 401(k) plan may make matching (optional) contributions to the plan of eligible employees on their behalf and to their benefit; employers may also add a profit-sharing feature to the plan. Earnings accrue on a tax-deferred basis.

2. **Bond** – A debt investment in which an investor lends money to a corporate or governmental entity which borrows the funds for a defined period of time. There can be either a variable or fixed interest rate. Bonds are used by companies, municipalities, states and sovereign governments to raise money and finance a variety of projects and activities. Owners of bonds are debtholders, or creditors, of the issuer.

3. **Common Stock** – This is what most retail or individual investors purchase. It represents a partial ownership interest – via "shares" – in a publicly traded or closely-held company.
4. **Correction** – A negative movement of at least 10% in a stock, bond, commodity or index to adjust for a perceived overvaluation. Corrections are generally temporary price declines interrupting an uptrend in the market or a specific financial instrument.
5. **DCA/Dollar Cost Averaging** – The technique of buying a fixed dollar amount of a particular investment on a regular schedule, regardless of the share price. More shares are purchased when prices are low (your fixed dollar amount goes farther), and fewer shares are bought when prices are high (your fixed dollars do not buy as many).
6. **Diversification** – A general technique for reducing investment risk. It is a risk management technique that mixes a wide variety of investments within a portfolio. If the asset values do not move up and down in perfect synchrony, a diversified portfolio will have less risk of loss than the weighted average risk of its components. A well-diversified portfolio often has less risk than the least risky asset within it. The rationale behind this technique is that a portfolio of different kinds of investments will, on average, yield higher returns and pose a lower risk than any individual investment found within the portfolio. Diversification thus strives to smooth out unsystematic risk events in a portfolio so that the positive performance of some investments will neutralize the negative performance of others. Therefore, the benefits of diversification will hold only if the securities in the portfolio are not perfectly correlated.
7. **ETF/Electronically Trade Funds** – An ETF is a marketable security that tracks an index, a commodity, bonds,

or a basket of assets like an index fund. Unlike mutual funds, an ETF trades like a common stock on a stock exchange. ETFs experience price changes throughout the day as they are bought and sold. ETFs typically have higher daily liquidity and lower fees than mutual fund shares, making them an attractive alternative for individual investors.

8. **Fair Value** – The estimated potential market price of a good, service, or asset (stock, etc.). It is both an accountancy and an economic measure. The fair value amount and the actual market price may be different, allowing an investor to determine that the good, service, or stock is advantageous or disadvantageous to purchase at that time.

9. **Fundamental Analysis** – The process of attempting to determine the fair market value of a security. This value is compared to the current market price to determine whether to buy, sell, or hold the security. Factors considered in fundamental analysis include the economic environment, the stock market environment, monetary policy, fiscal policy, interest rates, business cycles, and industry trends. Types of fundamental analysis include a top-down analysis, bottom-up analysis, and ratio analysis (liquidity, activity, profitability, and debt ratios). Bottom-up approach – analyzes, in order, a specific company, a specific industry, then the economy to identify a security for purchase by an investor. Top-down approach – analyzes, in order, the economy, the specific industry, then the specific company to identify a security for purchase and investor.

10. **Index or Indices** – A statistical measure of change in an economy or a securities market. In the case of financial markets, an index is a portfolio of securities representing

a particular market or a portion of it; examples include the S&P500, Wilshire5000, and any ETF. Each index has its own calculation methodology and is usually expressed in terms of a change from a base value. Thus, the percentage change is more important than the actual numeric value.

11. **Intrinsic Value** – The actual value of a company or an asset, based on an underlying perception of its true value. True value would include all aspects of the business, in terms of both tangible and intangible factors, and may or may not correspond exactly to its current market price.

12. **IRA** – An investing and/or saving plan used by individuals to earn and earmark funds for retirement savings. Like the 401(k), the Tax Code defines and manages taxation, which is done a bit differently according to the types of IRA: Traditional IRAs, Roth IRAs, SIMPLE IRAs and SEP IRAs.

13. **Large Cap Stock** – A term used by the investment community to refer to companies with a market capitalization value of more than $10 billion. Capitalization is a dollar value calculated by the number of shares issued times the price of a share. Large cap is an abbreviation of the term "large market capitalization".

14. **Main Street** – Idiomatic term used to refer to individual investors, employees with retirement or other investment accounts, and the general economy they participate in.

15. **Market Capitalization** – A value calculated by multiplying the number of a company's shares issued in the financial markets by the price of one share.

16. **Modern Portfolio Theory (MPT)** – A theory on how risk-averse investors can construct a portfolio to optimize or maximize expected return based on a given level of

market risk, emphasizing that risk is an inherent part of higher reward.

17. **Mutual Fund** – A mutual fund is an investment in a set group of assets which generally have an area of focus (all bonds, all real estate, all in overseas markets, all in energy, etc.). The riskier the area the fund invests in, the greater the potential gain or loss. Mutual funds are operated by money managers, who invest the fund's capital and attempt to produce capital gains and income for the fund's investors.

18. **Options** – A financial derivative that represents a contract sold by one party (option writer) to another party (option holder). A stock option is the most commonly known. Contrary to the underlying stock, an option has a limited lifespan during which action must be taken by the holder. The contract offers the option buyer the right, but not the obligation, to buy or sell a security or other financial asset at an agreed-upon price during a certain period of time or on a definite date (exercise date).

19. **Portfolio** – A grouping of an individual's (or a company's) financial assets such as stocks, bonds and cash equivalents, as well as their mutual, exchange traded and closed-fund counterparts. Portfolios are held directly by investors and/or managed by financial professionals.

20. **Registered Investment Advisor (RIA)** – An advisor or firm of advisors engaged in the investment advisory business and registered either with the Securities and Exchange Commission (SEC) or state securities authorities. A Registered Investment Advisor is defined by The Investment Advisors Act of 1940 as a "person or firm that, for compensation, is engaged in the act of providing advice, making recommendations, issuing reports or furnishing analyses on securities, either directly or through

publications." An investment advisor has a *fiduciary duty* to his or her clients, which means that the advisor has an obligation to provide suitable investment advice and always act in the clients' best interests.

21. **Risk** – The chance that an investment's actual return will be different from expectations or hopes. Risk includes the possibility of losing some or all of the original investment. Different versions of risk are usually measured by calculating the standard deviation of the historical returns or average returns of a specific investment. A high standard deviation indicates a high degree of risk.

22. **Risk Management** – The process of identification, analysis and either acceptance or mitigation of uncertainty in investment decision-making. Essentially, risk management occurs anytime an investor or portfolio manager analyzes and attempts to quantify the potential for loss in an investment and then takes the appropriate action (or inaction) given their investment objectives and risk tolerance. Inadequate risk management can result in severe consequences for companies as well as individuals.

23. **Separately Managed Account** – An account where 100% of the value of the account is owned by the investor who has hired a professional money manager to manage investments within the account using an asset-based fee structure.

24. **SCA – Strategic Cost Averaging**™ – The technique of buying a non-fixed dollar amount of a particular investment on an irregular schedule, only when the share price drops. Shares are purchased only when prices are low, and no shares are bought when prices are high.

25. **Small Cap Stock** – Refers to stocks with a fairly small market capitalization; this "capitalization" value is calculated by the dollar value of the share times the number of shares issued. The definition of small cap companies can

vary, but generally indicates those capitalized between $300 million and $2 billion.

26. **Stock** – Type of security that signifies ownership ("shares" or "equity") in a corporation and represents a claim on part of the corporation's assets and earnings.

27. **Style Box** – Defined by Morningstar, a style box is designed to visually symbolize the investment characteristics of fixed income, domestic stock and international stock securities and their corresponding mutual funds. A style box is a valuable tool for investors to use to determine the asset allocation and risk-return structures of their portfolios and/or how a security fits into their investing criteria. There are slightly different style boxes used for equities and fixed-income funds.

28. **Systematic Risk** – Market risk which is both unpredictable and impossible to completely avoid. It cannot be mitigated through diversification; it is the risk inherent to an entire market. Systematic risk, also known as "undiversifiable risk," "volatility" or "market risk," affects the overall market, not just a particular stock or industry.

29. **Tax Efficient Portfolio** – A portfolio in which structure and operations are based on reducing the tax liability that the portfolio owner may face. Reducing the tax liability of a portfolio is done in three main ways: a) By purchasing tax-free (or low taxed) investments such as municipal bonds. b) Keeping the portfolio's turnover low, especially if the portfolio invests in common stock. Holding stocks for more than one year, as they are taxed at a lower long-term capital gains rate than short-term transactions. c) Avoiding or limiting income-generating assets, such as dividend-paying stocks, which create a tax liability at each dividend issuance.

30. **Technical Analysis** – Technical analysis is an attempt to determine the value of securities through an analysis of the

historic market activity, such as past trading prices and volume. Technical analysis does not attempt to measure a security's intrinsic value. Instead, it is believed that by analyzing past activity (trades) of a security (trotting) along with sentiment, flow of funds, and market structure indicators, future movement of price of a security can be predicted.

33. **Volatility** – Essentially, the opposite of stability. Prices may be both stable (for a period) and volatile (for a period), in reaction to outside stimuli. Commonly, the higher the volatility, the riskier the security. It is a statistical measure of the dispersion of returns for a given security or market index. Volatility can either be measured by using the standard deviation or variance between returns from that same security or market index.

34. **Wall Street** – A street in lower Manhattan that is the original home of the *NYSE*. The street is the historic headquarters of the largest U.S. brokerages and investment banks. Many have since relocated to other areas of Manhattan and the USA. <u>Historical note</u>: *Wall Street* was named after the wooden wall that Dutch colonists built in this area in 1653 to defend themselves from the British and Native Americans.

35. **Wire house** – An archaic term used to describe a financial broker-dealer. Modern-day wire houses can range from small local brokerages to huge institutions with offices around the world. <u>Historical note</u>: The term "wire house" owes its origins to the fact that prior to the advent of modern wireless communications, brokerage firms were connected to their branches chiefly through telephone and telegraph wires. This enabled branches to have access to the same market information as the head office, thus allowing their brokers to provide stock quotes and market news to their clients.

END NOTES

i.   James Montier, 'Little Book on Behavioral Investing'

ii.   Benjamin Graham, 'The Intelligent Investor'

iii.   http://www.businessinsider.com/

iv.   "Flash Boys: A Wall Street Revolt" (W.W. Norton and Co.)

v.   The Greatest Investors: Philip Fisher | Investopedia http://www.investopedia.com/university/greatest/philipfisher.asp#ixzz3sezWhEtu

vi.   INVESTOPEDIA

vii.   Edwin J. Elton and Martin J. Gruber, 'MPT and Investment Analysis'

viii.   Quantitative Analysis Of Investor Behavior

ix.   Benjamin Graham, 'The Intelligent Investor'

x.   Excerpt from Peter Lynch & John Rothschild, 'Beating the Street'

xi.   http://www.jamesaltucher.com/2014/04/the-ultimate-cheat-sheet-for-investing-all-of-your-money/

xii.   'The Kiasu Way of Investing: The correlation between volatility and returns'; November 28 MoneyMind.sg

xiii.   Warren Buffett

xiv.   Professor of Finance at the Wharton School of the University of Pennsylvania

xv.   Based on ICON Advisors' research, "The Problematic Style Grid" by Charles Howard, July 2005

xvi.   Drescher Kleinwort Wasserstein "Seven Deadly Sins of Money Managers" and developed by Dr. KW Macro and Bogle, 2005

xvii. Comparing income with peers causes unhappiness By Emma Wilkinson Health reporter, BBC News 29 May 2010

xviii. Allan Roth, "Addiction Prediction" April 1, 2012 Financial Planning Magazine; Allan S. Roth is founder of the planning firm Wealth Logic in Colorado Springs, Colo., and writes the Irrational Investor column for CBS MoneyWatch.com. He is an adjunct faculty member at the University of Denver.

xix.   Tom Dorsey Dorsey and Associates

xx.   John Maynard Keynes, "The General Theory of Employment, Interest and Money"
       xiv http://www.pauleyfinancial.com/april-2012

www.ingramcontent.com/pod-product-compliance
Lightning Source LLC
Chambersburg PA
CBHW041146210326

41519CB00046B/136